India Macroeconomics Annual
2007

India Macroeconomics Annual
2007

Editor
Sugata Marjit

SAGE Los Angeles • London • New Delhi • Singapore
www.sagepublications.com

First published in 2008 by

SAGE Publications India Pvt Ltd
B1/I-1 Mohan Cooperative Industrial Area
Mathura Road
New Delhi 110 044, India
www.indiasage.com

SAGE Publications Inc
2455 Teller Road
Thousand Oaks, California 91320, USA

SAGE Publications Ltd
1 Oliver's Yard, 55 City Road
London EC1Y 1SP, United Kingdom

SAGE Publications Asia-Pacific Pte Ltd
33 Pekin Street
#02-01 Far East Square, Singapore 048763

Published by Vivek Mehra for SAGE Publications India Pvt Ltd, typeset in 10/13 Aldine401 BT and printed at Chaman Enterprises, New Delhi.

ISSN: 0–973–290–X
ISBN: 978–81–7829–871–9 (India-Pb)

The SAGE Team: Sugata Ghosh, Vaijayantee Bhattacharya, Anju Saxena

Contents

Contents

Editorial Board

Editor's Note

We are happy to bring out the current issue of *India Macroeconomics Annual 2007*, a joint venture of the Centre for Studies in Social Sciences, Calcutta and SAGE Publications India Pvt Ltd. This is the fourth issue of the annual partly funded by the Reserve Bank of India Endowment at the Centre for Studies in Social Sciences, Calcutta. We are also happy to inform the readers that *India Macroeconomics Annual* is now listed under the AEA Electronic Indexes, which are included in JEL on CD, *e-JEL* and EconLit.

The views expressed in the articles belong entirely to the authors and in no way implicate the Reserve Bank of India.

Sugata Marjit
Centre for Studies in Social Sciences, Calcutta

Section I

Section I

The Labour Market in India: A Survey of Some Contemporary Issues

SAIBAL KAR
Centre for Studies in Social Sciences, Calcutta

This section deals with a number of issues that has found significant presence in earlier and more recent discussions on the labour market in India, which, despite their regional emphases, have strong implications for economies of similar types. These include the wage and employment patterns in the formal sector, the labour market reforms and the unregulated or informal sector. The unifying thread for the entire analysis is drawn on the question of whether the labour market reforms in India shall have a palpable impact on the organized sector and how the unorganized counterpart would cope with such changes, especially in relation to the broader question facing the manufacturing and service industries.

JEL Classification: J21, J31, J8
Keywords: Labour reform, Wages, Employment, Unorganized sector, India

1. Introduction

Certain issues in the Indian labour market continue to draw attention and emphasis starting from the early post-colonial decades. Albeit, in the recent years, the focus and directionality associated with these issues have shifted significantly, conclusive answers to many of those as well as the more recent ones have largely eluded the concerned mass. Consequently, policy formulations aimed at resolving the apparent paradoxes and puzzles present in the labour market have been imprecise and only partially effective. Consider, for example, the wage-employment relation in the Indian labour market on which volumes have been written and several features have been discussed. And yet, the contemporary research agendas find this area still appealing, not only because newer issues have come up, but also because the older debate has not yielded satisfactory answers. In fact, the onset of the economic reforms and the changing face of the labour market, with lesser and lesser interventions by either the government or the labour unions, have made the issues rather complicated and intricately related with many other factors not controlled for in most previous studies. Consequently, the newer genre of studies on wage-employment patterns in India regularly reflect the concerns of the present times, that is, the post-reform era when the economic reforms in general have virtually opened up a Pandora's box. While a clearer picture would certainly be available when the dust settles, what this period of reconstruction offers is not negligible. In view of some of these findings, this section offers a brief survey of the most recent literature, thereby shelving the older issues on the evolving wage-employment patterns in India for comparison at a suitable point in future.

It has also been well-established by now that any debate on the wage-employment relationship, which earlier centred predominantly around the formal or organized sector, would be rather incomplete without an attempt to understand the contemporary process of labour market reforms in India. The implications of the labour market reform on the formal or organized sector, then, distinctly point towards recasting the debate after suitable inclusion of the informal or unorganized sector, which turns out to be one of the most dynamic elements within the labour market. Thus, in Section 2, we discuss the intricacies of the labour market reforms in India with wide-ranging implications for the industrial sector in the country. This offers a contemporary view of the policy debate on a rather controversial issue in India, and creates a space for re-evaluating some of the questions that assumed centre stage in the long dialogues on the wage-employment relations. In Section 3, we engage in a fresh discussion on the conditions of wage and employment in the unorganized sector in India. The unifying factor in the entire analysis revolves around the question of whether the labour market reforms in India would have a palpable impact on the organized sector and how its unorganized counterpart cope with such changes, especially in relation to the evolving manufacturing and service industries. The increased informalization and casualization of the labour force in India and many other developing countries also generate a universal appeal to the question of labour market reforms.

1.1 Wages and Employment in the Organized Sector

One of the most interesting questions in the face of economic liberalization in India has been the flexibility of formal wages and its implications for the level of employment. It is simple to understand that if the fall in labour supply in response to wage cut outweighs the increase in the demand for labour due to falling wages, then the level of employment must fall. It is possible in agglomeration economies that some regions display a situation wherein the downsizing of the formal sector and loss of productivity actually translate into job losses or wage cuts or both. It may also be the case that in some other pockets, there might be a strong inducement towards higher employment and higher wages, leading to prevalence of wide disparities both in the labour market and in the economy, in general. In fact, Mitra (2006) constructs the present concerns in the labour market to argue that there may even be another case, where the total factor productivity (TFP) growth leads to simultaneous improvements in the growth elements, real wages and employment in some regions of the country. In this connection, Mitra (2006) also estimates the growth rates in wages and employment by selecting two sub-periods during the pre- and post-reform decades in India: that is, 1979–80 to 1990–91 and 1990–91 to 1997–98. He measures the exponential growth patterns by fitting a semi-logarithmic trend equation to each variable [gross value added/employee, wage/worker, fixed capital/employee, gross fixed capital formation, man-hours, and so forth, as available from the Annual Survey of Industries (ASI)] across industry classification ranging between categories 20–21 and 38, and found that the rate of growth of workers at the all-India level corresponding to the ASI sector increased during the second period as compared to the first [except for industry types 29 (leather) and 32 (non-metallic)]. Earlier, in a related vein, Nagaraj (1994), observed that the earnings per worker grew faster than the per capita income during the 1980s mainly due to an increase in the number of man-days/worker. More recently, Tendulkar (2004) notes that the organized labour market in India is under a state of churning, especially during the reform period, as the formal rules incorporated in the protective labour legislation continue to persist, despite its inability to protect employment in the face of growing domestic and foreign competition. It comes as no surprise that the cross-currents of protective schemes and the constant search by the employers to switch to cost saving techniques, including resorting to flexible labour allocation modes and outsourcing to sectors where the labour laws are less stringent, creates a state of redundancy .

   Mitra (2006) further shows that the rate of increase in fixed capital and employment across the industry types previously mentioned are positively correlated (though modestly), implying that the technical advancements that brought in faster capital accumulation did not do so necessarily at the cost of employment. The brief venture, so far, clearly establishes that the case of the labour market cannot be treated in isolation and that the legal aspects along with proper institutional arrangements must be factored in so as to produce any meaningful estimate of the contemporaneous or future conditions. In fact, for the benefit of labour productivity to percolate down to the workers, it is imperative that the social security network, health benefits, old-age benefits, unemployment benefits or unemployment insurance—all these must be serious agendas in the issue of labour market reform. Mitra (2006) argues that the situation is complicated further by the presence of labour contractors, who regularly draw a section of the workers' pay or other benefits receivable as rents. The reform agendas, as discussed in the next section, take no cognizance of these issues in asymmetric information and moral hazard problems prevalent in the labour market and hindering a smooth functioning of the same.

2. Labour Market Reforms in India[1]

The concept of labour market reforms in India is in its nascent stage, and consequently, despite frequent debates in various forums on this issue, little or no progress has been witnessed in recent times. In the Economic Survey 2005–06 (Ministry of Finance, Government of India 2006), the Ministry of Finance noted:

> Various studies indicate that Indian labour laws are highly protective of labour, and labour markets are relatively inflexible. These laws apply only to the organised sector. Consequently, these laws have restricted labour mobility, have led to capital-intensive methods in the organised sector and adversely affected the sector's long-run demand for labour. Labour being a subject in the concurrent list, State-level labour regulations are also an important determinant of industrial performance. Evidence suggests that States, which have enacted more pro-worker regulations, have lost out on industrial production in general. (p. 209)

It is probably well-known by now that the views put forward in these lines are constituted from the basic findings of Besley and Burgess (2004), which essentially show that provinces like Gujarat, Maharashtra, Orissa and West Bengal, which enacted pro-worker legislations, were also the states with high incidence of informal activities as compared to states that were classified as

---

[1] This sub-section is co-authored with Bibhas Saha, Department of Economics, University of East Anglia, UK.

pro-employer. While the former experienced low industrial growth, declining formal productivity, and so forth, the pro-employer states reported positive growth in most of these aspects. Some of the contemporary studies also used the Besley and Burgess (2004) formulation to re-classify the states according to the initial labour laws constituted with subsequent amendments (Hasan et al. 2003), and to establish that trade reforms increase the own price elasticity of demand more vigorously in the states where the labour market is more flexible. However, it turns out that the classification scheme selected for the states—irrespective of whether they are pro-labour, pro-employer or inflexible labour markets—plays a crucial role in guiding the outcomes. Not surprisingly, there is a contemporaneous body of literature on the subject which subscribes to a different viewpoint, especially with regard to the Industrial Disputes Act of 1976 and 1982 (for a review of the empirical literature, see Bhattacharjea 2006). Clearly, therefore, there is a case for re-evaluating the normative concerns of the labour market flexibility on sound theoretical and empirical grounds. What is attempted in this sub-section, however, is another look at the state of the labour laws and regulations in India that can have a significant influence on the industrial situation in the country, especially at a time when the waning labour union memberships and substantial informalization of the labour force dominate the labour market.

It has been well-established at this point that much of the Indian reform programme has concentrated on industrial and trade policies. The most important changes, so far, have been the removal of licensing, de-reservation of small scale industries, phased reduction of tariff rates, shortening of the negative list for export, welcoming of foreign investment and, above all, curbing of the monopoly of the public sector in almost all industries. Capital and foreign exchange markets have also been significantly liberalized. However, very little has changed in the area of labour laws and labour regulations, and to use the terms of Nagaraj (2007),

> Like in many developing economies, in India too, labor legislations tend to be aspirational with limited effectiveness, in the absence of a credible enforcement mechanism. Ambiguity in the legal system leaves considerable discretion to the administration and to the judiciary that could be detrimental to the smooth function of the labor market. (p. 5)

Considering that labour laws have direct implications for the industrial sector, the sluggish pace of the implementation of reforms has attracted attention from many quarters, and the political and judicial concerns acting in favour or against the process cannot be completely neglected if one has to understand the normative implications of any reform in a populist democracy like India. Let us begin with the state of the labour laws in India.

2.1 Labour Laws in India

2.1.1 *The Factories Act*

This Act, which came into effect in 1948, essentially defined and categorized the industrial workers in India; the Shops and Establishments Act, a state legislation, did the same for the services sector. The Factories Act is intended to protect the safety and working conditions and mandates registration of all factories employing 10 or more workers using power on a regular basis (20 or more workers without using power). The mandated benefits for workers—Provident Fund, gratuity, provision of food in the workplace, and so forth, as defined under the Factories Act—increase with the factory size. In fact, the concept of industrial relations in India is regulated by three major Central Acts, namely:

(i) The Industrial Employment (Standing Orders) Act, 1946 (henceforth IE).
(ii) The Trade Union Act, 1926 (henceforth TU).
(iii) The Industrial Disputes Act, 1947 (henceforth IDA). Following are brief descriptions of each of these Acts.

2.1.2 *The Industrial Employment (IE) (Standing Orders) Act*

The IE Act requires that the status of an industrial employee, along with the conditions of recruitment, confirmation, misconduct, discharge, disciplinary action, leave, holidays, and so forth, be explained to the employee by the employer in the most precise terms. The Act applies to the whole of India and to all industrial establishments employing 50 workers or more. The Act also provides for severance pay.

2.1.3 *The Trade Union (TU) Act*

The TU Act, on the other hand, is one of the few labour laws that has remained almost unchanged since the pre-Independence period. The Act recognizes workers' freedom of association to express grievances, to engage in collective bargaining, and to pursue civil and political interests among themselves. A union requires at least seven members for registration, and it can be formed at the factory level as well as at the industry level. Half of the office bearers of a union must be engaged in the industry to which the union belongs. One of the crucial provisions of the Act is that the union members and office bearers are protected from criminal and civil suits in relation to bona fide trade union activities.[2]

While this Act has been seen as the hallmark of trade unionism, very little has been done to revise it in the light of the changed circumstances. The Act is so general that it views participation in a political strike as being as legitimate as participation in an industrial strike. There are other difficulties, as the law is not particularly helpful in reducing the multiplicity of unions with conflicting agendas and viewpoints or in identifying the legitimate negotiating authority.

In the planning era, trade unions also grew in strength largely, in order to capture a share of the rent generated by import substitution policies. Large powerful unions with strong political affiliations were a common occurrence. In the post-liberalization era, collective bargaining has taken a more decentralized character. With fewer governmental controls and steady disappearance of trade barriers, the unions' need to maintain strong political links has certainly waned. Consequently, the entire nexus of trade unions and political parties with which they sought affiliation was significantly weakened.

2.1.4 *The Industrial Disputes Act (IDA)*

Any dispute on terms and conditions of work, or disagreements during negotiations over wage or any other matter come under the purview of the IDA. Enacted in 1947, this Act replaced the Trade Disputes Act of 1929. The IDA became the main governing legislation with respect to industrial relations all over the country. As its importance grew over time, several amendments were passed in 1964, 1965, 1971, 1976, 1982 and 1984 to improve upon its shortcomings and also to strengthen the interventionist role of the state.

The Act aimed to create a legal and regulatory framework within which industrial disputes can be peacefully resolved. Among the main provisions of the Act are:

(i) Defining the legality of strikes and lockouts,
(ii) Restrictive procedure for layoffs, retrenchment and closure,
(iii) Compensation for layoff and retrenchment,
(iv) Conciliation procedure and
(v) A three-tier system of adjudication.

---

[2] See Table 3 for trends in TU membership between 1987–2001.

The legality of a strike or lockout primarily hinges on the question of fair use.[3] For example, a sudden strike or lockout[4] is illegal in public utilities and prior notice must be served. The employers or employees are expected to inform the labour commissioner before declaring a lockout or going on a strike. In all such disputes, the labour commissioner is, in principle, a party to the decisions. In all industries, when a dispute is under conciliation or adjudication, a fresh strike or lockout is illegal, but continuance of the old strike or lockout can be legal. On the other hand, a strike or lockout in retaliation of an illegal lockout or illegal strike is perfectly legal. It is also important that a striking employee must qualify as a 'workman' as defined in the Act, which means that:

(i) His wage must be below a certain level,
(ii) He should not be a contract worker and
(iii) He should not be a manager or supervisor.

Rules regarding lay-off, retrenchment and closure of a unit are far more restrictive. The IE Act permits certain types of layoffs (as contractual) or retrenchment (on disciplinary or medical grounds). But if a layoff is instigated by financial reasons, then IDA comes into force. Since 1976, the IDA has made it *mandatory* for employers to seek prior permission from the government to lay off or retrench any worker, or close down the unit.[5] Besides, in the organized sector, workers are entitled to severance of pay at the rate of half a month's salary for every year worked.

While large firms generally face more restraints with regard to their preferred wage-employment practices, relatively smaller firms can freely lay off or retrench in compliance with the IE Act (wherever it is applicable). In the event of retrenchment, the principle of 'last come, first go' applies. However, not all laid-off or retrenched workers are eligible for compensation;

[3] The Act states, 'No person employed in a public utility service shall go on strike in breach of contract, without giving to the employer notice of strike, as hereinafter provided, within six weeks before striking or within fourteen days of giving such notice'. A strike or lockout shall be illegal if it is commenced or declared in contravention of Section 22 or Section 23 or it is continued in contravention of an order made under Sub-section (3) of Section 10 [or Sub-section (4A) of Section 10A]. The Act states, 'No person shall knowingly expend or apply any money in direct furtherance or support of any illegal strike or lockout', thus prohibiting financial aid to illegal strikes. Penalty for illegal strikes and lockouts ranges from a one-month prison term to monetary fines of one thousand rupees.

[4] Lockout is a temporary closure of plant by managements when their negotiations with workers' unions fail. It is a mirror image of a strike by workers.

[5] Private firms have to seek permission from the state government, and the central public sector units (PSUs) from the Central Government.

only the permanent workers are eligible for compensation and that too only when the firm employs more than 50 people.

Finally, it is noteworthy that the enforcement of the ID and IE Acts is primarily the state governments' responsibility, which typically brings up the issue discussed at the beginning of this sub-section. The states are also empowered to pass enabling legislations within the framework of the Central Acts. Most states have indeed amended the ID Act many times to address the local concerns. Researchers believe that these amendments have largely reflected the state governments' activism and ideology on labour issues. Some states such as Andhra Pradesh have made changes in favour of the employers, while quite a few others like West Bengal have favoured the workers .[6] Table 1 shows the average number of man-days lost, average number of workers involved per disputes, and so forth, during 2001–04. The trend seems to indicate that the average time loss per dispute is still steadily rising in India.

2.1.5 *Industrial Relations*

Given the complex and divergent nature of labour legislations, it is not surprising that the Indian industry has long been plagued by disputes. Although there is an elaborate procedure of dispute resolution, in practice, the system has been extremely inefficient. Industrial disputes had steadily risen from a moderate level in the late 1960s to new heights in the mid-1970s and early 1980s, and then gradually by the 1990s, it took a back seat. Over these four decades, two visible jumps were observed for the man-days lost. The year 1976 registered a very low occurrence of strikes and lockouts, while 1982 was the peak year. The much improved disputes scenario of recent times is, however, entirely due to a steadily declining trend in strikes, which has effectively counteracted the rising trend in lockouts (which are often suspected to be disguised attempts to exit). The divergence in the trends of strikes and lockouts has started from the mid-1980s. A negative feature shared by both strikes and lockouts is that, on an average, each type of dispute causes greater loss in terms of man-days. Generally, the private sector witnesses more disputes, but obviously the scale of operation is far below the employment capacity in most public sector units.

It is perhaps not beyond general comprehension that the regulatory institutions for labour have often worked on conflicting purposes, mostly influenced as they are by variations in the way the labour laws were endorsed

---

[6] For example, in 1987, Andhra Pradesh failed to comply with an order by the state government constraining disputes as a punishable offence. Although this applies to both workers and employers, in practice, it has a greater impact on the workers. On the other hand, West Bengal passed many pro-worker Acts. For example, in 1980, it made prior payment of compensation to the worker a precondition for closure, though the Central ID Act does not require so.

TABLE 1

Average time loss/workers involved per dispute and average number of man-days lost per worker due to industrial disputes in India (2000–2004)

Year/Item	All industries	Manufacturing industries	Mining and quarrying	Crops and horticulture
2000				
Average no. of workers involved per disputes (workers)	1864	1721	4399	727
Average no. of man-days lost per worker involved (days)	25	34	4	44
2001				
Average time loss per disputes (man-days)	35262	47748	12906	29008
2002				
Average time loss per disputes (man-days)	45917	59050	18216	31741
2003				
Average no. of man-days lost per worker involved (days)	35	89	4	39
Average time loss per dispute (man-days)	54811	49967	331868	60754
Average no. of workers involved per dispute (workers)	3290	1321	34380	5376
2004				
Average no. of man-days lost per worker involved (days)	17	38	10	11
Average time loss per dispute (man-days)	50034	56227	103825	46260
Average no. of workers involved per dispute (workers)	4344	1353	15259	1211
Average no. of man-days lost per worker involved (days)	12	42	7	38

Source: Industrial Disputes in India, Ministry of Labour and Employment, Government of India, Various Issues.

or opposed at the state level. The central legislations also use variable thresholds to enforce different provisions and regulations. For example, the IDA makes layoff compensation mandatory in all firms employing 50 or more workers, but the permission to lay off is to be sought only if the firm size exceeds 100 workers. The various economic implications of the asymmetric treatment of units by the state and central authorities certainly offer future agendas for research in this context.

2.2 Implications of Labour Market Rigidity

Analytically speaking, the existence of labour laws, their enforcement, regulation and trade union practices—all interactively create a perception among investors about the flexibility of the labour market. Lower flexibility translates into greater cost of employment, which may induce the investors to shy away, or employ fewer workers. Ironically, governments in developing countries often strategically use pro-worker labour laws as a substitute for non-existent or poor social security programmes and in effect, shift the welfare burden onto the firms. However, much of this burden comes back in the form of tax foregone and production subsidies offered to attract investment.

Researchers try to measure rigidity by suitable indices that combine various aspects of the labour market. In a recent paper, Klapper et al. (2005) compare the level of labour market rigidities in India and China to find that it is 3.33 times more in India than in China. Here, we summarize the implications of labour rigidity in Indian industries mainly with a view to revisit the puzzle of 'jobless growth' (also see Sharma 2006). In fact, despite the acceleration of economic growth close to 6 per cent on a trend basis over the last quarter century, and the recent flare of about 9 per cent GDP growth, the employment growth has remained more or less stagnant at a mere 0.69 per cent. While it implies rapid labour productivity growth, it has also meant insufficient creation of employment opportunities in the so-called formal or organized sector. It is documented in several recent publications that the burden of job creation, irrespective of however miniscule and deficient at the individual unit levels it might be, has been borne largely by the unorganized sector in India. A comparison of the GDP growth and employment growth is available in Table 2. Although the industrial output has always grown much faster than the industrial employment, the gap widened the most between 1980 and 1990.[7] Moreover, between 1997 and 2004, the organized sector cut back

---

[7] It is argued that the policy of import substitution, which favoured capital-intensive industries, and discriminated against labour-intensive traditional (primary product-based) industries, contributed most towards this effect. Other policy measures also implied an adverse or distorted wage-rental ratio that led to relatively greater application of capital than labour. See Lucas (1988) and particularly Mookherjee (1995, pp.14–15) for more on this.

1.8 million (6.3 per cent) jobs, mostly in manufacturing (1.2 million jobs or 18 per cent) (Ministry of Finance, Government of India, 2006). Consequently, the space for the jobless puzzle, that is, the co-existence of high economic growth with insufficient employment opportunities, drew enormous attention from all quarters.

TABLE 2

Average growth rates for India (per cent)

	Real value added of industry (output)	Registered manufacturing employment	Real GDP
1960–70	6.86	3.68	3.82
1970–80	4.59	4.00	3.15
1980–90	8.37	0.60	5.67
1990–97	9.30	2.58	4.6*
1960–90	6.25	2.69	4.15

Data Sources: Annual Survey of Industries (ASI), National Accounts Statistics.
Source: Saha (2006).
Note: *For 1990–95.

During the past decade, there have also been a few interesting exchanges with regard to the causes of labour market rigidity in India. For example, Nagaraj (1994), supported by Bhalotra (1998), disapproved of the explanation provided by the World Bank that job security provisions resulted in sluggish employment generation trends and added to the labour market rigidities. The question of rigidity in the Indian labour market actually received a more careful attention in Fallon and Lucas (1991, 1993), and the results partially support the World Bank's view that job security regulation reduced long-run employment by 17.5 per cent on the aggregate level though it did not significantly affect the speed of employment adjustment, that is, there was no change in the adjustment cost.

However, the last point of Fallon and Lucas has been contradicted by Bhalotra (1998) and Dutta Roy (2003). Both have argued that the estimated loss of employment was exaggerated, because this loss was found to be significant in only 11 out of 35 industries studied by Fallon and Lucas. Nevertheless, if we confine our attention only to those industries where job losses were econometrically significant, we see that, according to the estimates of Fallon and Lucas, the cotton textile industry suffered a loss of 36.1 per cent employment, soaps and cosmetics—33.3 per cent, silk and synthetics—44.8 per cent, plastics—18.5 per cent and railway equipments—19.6 per cent.

In brief, therefore, the above studies produce significant evidence on two types of problems: employment adjustment costs and probable loss of employment through a shift of the labour demand curve for some industries. But as far as the adjustment costs are concerned, they were probably not worsened by the job security legislation. This does not seem to be inconsistent with theoretical predictions that various types of regulations work in various ways, with some of them counteracting each other.

2.3 The Post-liberalization Period

It is widely accepted that despite a common stand on the urgency of bringing about labour reforms in India or at least some degree of rationalization, no significant moves have as yet been taken mainly due to lack of political consensus in a fractious democracy like India. It is not hard to believe that the cross-currents of economic and political interests continuously obfuscating the true agendas in the country might as well lead to policies that are undesirable on several grounds. Nevertheless, Nagaraj (2007) argues that this lack of inaction, perhaps, characterizes the so-called 'reform by stealth' where administrative means are applied to dilute the strength of laws, and with the consequent weakening of the bargaining power of trade unions, it has granted employers a greater freedom in their practice of industrial relations. While these arguments may have some merit in understanding the post-liberalization labour market practices in India, it is at best incomplete in judging the forces of globalization that have complicated situations far beyond such simple comprehension. The opening up of the domestic market to foreign competition, skill-based technological changes, high mobility of capital across various sectors in the country, and above all, the phenomenal expansion of the service sector have rendered the organized labour movement in India time-inconsistent (see Table 3). Furthermore, there is need to investigate and understand the causal relation between the two types of reforms and the welfare implications of implementing both, either contemporaneously or with strategic time lags. In fact, for India, the only possible choice in this regard is to implement the labour reforms after the trade reforms, now that a substantial period of time has elapsed since the onset of the first. It should be an interesting exercise to analyze the wage-employment conditions that would prevail under the changing circumstances.

Let us briefly report on two papers that study the counter-factuals, that is, the possible effects of not carrying out labour reforms. Aghion et al. (2005) applied the Besley–Burgess classification of states to examine the unequal effects of industrial and trade reforms across states in the manufacturing sector. They find that in comparison to the neutral states, the relative effects of industrial de-regulation have been significantly positive for those states

TABLE 3

Trade union membership in India (1987 to 2001)

Year	Workers' unions			Employers' unions			All unions		
	On register	Submitting returns	Membership of submitting returns ('000)	On register	Submitting returns	Membership of submitting ('000)	On register	Submitting returns	Membership of submitting returns ('000)
1987	48529	10953	7935	800	110	24	49329	11063	7959
1988	49255	8668	7055	793	62	18	50048	8730	7073
1989	51449	9674	9262	761	84	33	52210	9758	9295
1990	50797	8386	6931	1219	442	88	52016	8828	7019
1991	52773	8351	6094	762	67	6	53535	8418	6100
1992	54885	9073	5739	795	92	8	55680	9165	5746
1993	54969	6776	3129	815	30	5	55784	6806	3134
1994	56044	6265	4093	828	12	1	56872	6277	4094
1995	57163	8048	6516	789	114	22	57952	8162	6538
1996	58206	7229	5594	782	13	7	58988	7242	5601
1997	59875	8774	7373	785	98	36	60660	8872	7409
1998	61199	7291	7229	1024	112	20	62223	7403	7249
1999	64040	8061	6394	777	91	13	64817	8152	6407
2000	65286	7231	5417	770	22	4	66056	7253	5420
2001	65264	5693	4454	1000	13	2	66264	5706	4456

Source: Ministry of Labour and Employment, Government of India.

Notes: 1. Totals in Membership of Submitting Returns for All Unions may not necessarily tally with the Totals of Membership of Submitting Returns for Workers' Unions Employers' Unions and All Unions due to rounding off in thousand.

2. In the case of those states that did not submit return for the concerned year, the figures of the previous year were repeated under the register for Workers' Unions and Employers' Unions.

which have amended the IDA in a pro-employer direction, and significantly negative for those states that have enacted pro-worker legislations. Although the effects of trade reform alone have been positive for all states, the effects, as channelled through the labour market, have been unequal, depending on the nature of their past labour legislations.

Further, Chaudhuri et al. (2006) examine the effects of the unionization rate, trade and industrial de-regulation on the number of factories. They find that greater unionization and increased wageshare of the organized workers (which might have resulted from the absence of labour reform) have restricted the growth of the number of factories. On the other hand, industrial policy reform has had a favourable effect and promoted competition. But trade liberalization has shown a negative impact on the number of factories, suggesting possible bankruptcy of inefficient domestic firms.

It would thus be an overstatement to attribute the lack of flexibility in the organized employment sector entirely to labour legislation, since a large part of such rigidities may also be explained by various other factors peculiar to the industrial and economic policies in general. The archaic banking practices in India, the credit constraints facing many mid-sized firms and the limited access to various financial intermediaries until very recently, should not be completely ignored while trying to understand the formal industrial capacities in generating employment.[8]

3. Informal Sector in Contemporary Research

There should be little doubt by now that the entire span of the above analysis strongly demands a reconsideration of the facts and features by including the large unorganized sector present in India. In fact, the importance of considering the informal sector in the economic analysis of a developing country is of significant importance, not only owing to its sheer size, but also because of the contributions it makes towards sustaining a large mass of the marginalized population. To be specific, in countries like India or Bangladesh, about 75–80 per cent of the total workforce is engaged in informal economic activities. This proportion rises to a towering 90 per cent if agriculture is included as part of informal activities, which is usually the case in all such countries. According to the World Development Report (2000), the percentage is about 70 per cent for countries in the Middle Eastern including Turkey, whereas in

[8] See Anant and Goswami (1995) for an analysis of industrial sickness in India.

the case of eastern European countries like Bulgaria, Hungary, Ukraine or the Czech Republic, about 45–50 per cent of the economically active population falls under this classification. For Latin America and the Caribbean countries, the proportion is almost 70 per cent. Given the huge percentage of people working outside the formal regulations and arrangements, it becomes imperative to revisit the effects of economic reforms in countries like India only after accommodating the unorganized sector.

For example, if any structural change affects the labour market of the economy, it will affect a large number of people working in the informal sector in broadly three ways. First, it might be channelled through the vertical linkage in production that exists between the formal and the informal sectors. If the formal sector is dependent on the informal sector for the supply of certain intermediate goods, the expansion or contraction of the formal industries should directly affect the informal production of those commodities. Consequently, the wage-employment situations must undergo significant changes. Similarly, any changes in the prevailing labour laws, applicable only to the workers in the organized sector, such as the Factories Act or IDA, and so forth (as discussed in detail in the previous section), or even newly construed international labour standards (such as sanctions against child labour) would send ripples in the informal sector through these vertical linkages. The effect may not be too localized or insignificant, given that a large number of formal units in India outsource several production stages to the unorganized sector. Second, any changes in the tariff and non-tariff barriers may directly affect the informal sector, when the informal sector produces a tradable good. International sanctions on commodities produced with the use of child labour or ban on tannery products subjecting animals to poor treatments may directly affect the level of informal activities. Third, the informal sector may be affected by the situations in the formal industries and the formal capital market even without a vertical linkage, if there is high mobility of physical capital between the two sectors. A drop in formal (bank) interest rates, tax on savings or a mere contraction of the formal sector might see a flight of capital from the formal to the informal segments of the economy. Obviously, the degree of capital mobility would depend on the elasticity of the relative rate of return to capital in the formal sector and the relative supply of capital in the same, vis-à-vis the informal counterpart. In a recent study (Marjit and Kar 2007), it has been shown that if such elasticity exceeds a critical level, it can cause an increase in the informal wage, when the formal sector contracts and releases labour that flows into the informal sector for survival. The other important factor, which needs further exploration, is the risk-return trade-off that can affect the mobility of capital from the formal to the informal sector. In fact, a clear understanding of these factors can influence the policy formulations on the behaviour of the capital market in a strong way.

With this brief introduction, we offer a survey of the wage-employment conditions in the informal sector in Section 3.1. The survey considers some partial equilibrium analysis from different developing countries, and we construct an aggregative view of the perspective from this limited scope. The reason why we do not frequently come across aggregative data and supporting analyses on the informal sector has a lot to do with the inherent nature of the sector. It is not only difficult to keep track of the economic activities of the unorganized workers engaged in various forms of employment ranging from very small manufacturing units to those engaged in services as roadside vendors, but on an aggregative sense, it is near impossible to construct a reliable data set. Moreover, a close association between the informal workers and displaced or surplus agricultural workers make it a problem of definition. Another reason obviously is the existence of a clandestine part of the informal activities, which may even take the form of illegal production and service units.

3.1 Wages and Employment in the Informal Sector

The effect of economic reform on the aggregate wage-employment pattern of the informal workers has been recently analyzed in Marjit and Kar (2007), and Kar and Marjit (2001). The first one develops a theoretical model to analyze the effects of trade reforms on the wages earned by the informal workers, and the theoretical structure embedded in a general equilibrium model aimed at capturing the aggregative picture is strongly supported by an empirical evidence on the informal wage movements in India. Interestingly, it is shown that a high degree of capital mobility between the formal and informal sectors increases the informal wage. A partial equilibrium version of this model indicates the case wherein the capital is sector-specific in the two formal and informal sectors under consideration and that the trade reform may actually lower the informal wage in the absence of capital mobility. On the empirical side of the issue, the study shows that for most provinces and union territories in India, the wages of the workers in the so-called Non-Directory Manufacturing Enterprises (NDMEs)[9] have grown by an average of about 10 per cent annually during the post-reform decades.

---

[9] As per definitions available in the National Sample Survey Organisation (NSSO), NDMEs refer to units employing less than or equal to five workers, as opposed to Own Account Manufacturing Enterprises (OAMEs) or self-employed units.

The growth of the real wage is significantly explained by the per unit annual growth of real fixed assets and the real value added in the informal sector. Also, it may not be a mere accident that this period of high growth of real fixed assets in the informal sector coincided with declining real fixed capital stock in the formal industries, reflected immediately in the post-liberalization data. The study uses the comparative capital accumulation picture as a proxy for capital mobility between the formal and the informal sectors.

The second study by Kar and Marjit (2001) constructed a three-sector model with the informal sector as an independent category and producing an import substitute. The article studies the welfare implications of trade reform in this set-up to conclude that trade liberalization can improve the welfare of those in the informal sector, if the change in formal employment plus the own price consumption elasticity in the informal sector exceed the cross price elasticity of substitution in consumption between the formal and the informal commodities. A tariff cut in this model thus redistributes income to 'outsiders' who do not receive the patronage of the labour unions. If protection for the output of the informal sector is withdrawn, formal employees gain. If the agricultural export price increases, the real income of those already employed in the formal and informal sectors goes down.

These and several other theoretical and empirical studies on the informal sector consider the prevalent definition of this category as being sufficiently comprehensive. The term 'informal sector' was initially coined by ILO (1972), to mean 'illicit or illegal activities by individuals operating outside the formal sphere or the purpose of evading taxation or regulatory burden'. Alternatively, it may be defined as 'very small enterprises that use low-technology models and do not refer to legal status' (Webster and Fidler 1996). Both definitions fit the characteristics of a large number of informal enterprises in the developing countries. Such enterprises are characterized by small number of workers, a limited extent to which the firm abides by the laws and regulations of the country, and a low level of capitalization. Since there is relatively little usage of capital, land or energy in this sector, the most important economic issue concerning the informal sector is the wage and employment dynamics.

In the Indian context, the labour composition and the size of employment in the informal sector have been earlier estimated by Mitra (1998), Mahadevia (1996) and others. Mitra (1998), for example, uses two categories as constituents of the informal sector:

(a) Employment in own account enterprises, and
(b) Employment in establishments of a size of one to nine workers.

Evidence from Kurukshetra and Singh (1999) shows how entrenched informal sector employment may be in the labour market of a developing country. The authors here calculate informal employment in India to be 365 million for the year 1993–94. Not surprisingly, the share of informal earnings in GDP of India during this period (Rs. 4,93,948 crores, 61.81 per cent)[10] exceeds the formal earnings share (Rs. 3,05,129 crores, 38.19 per cent). Although gross earnings in the informal sector increased to Rs. 7,74,659 crores in the subsequent period, its share in GDP (60.27 per cent) fell a little below the previous level.

In a more recent article, Zagha (1998) traces the connection between economic liberalization and labour market situations in post-1991 India. According to him, even before the liberalization was undertaken in 1991, India had developed exceptionally complex labour regulations that strengthened the bargaining power of unions and increased job security in the formal economy at the cost of employment. In his article, it is suggested that de-regulation and privatization can be expected to strengthen competition, accelerate productivity growth, narrow the gaps between informal and formal earnings and weaken union power. Empirical evidence from this article shows that increased competition in product markets and dissipation of rents are eroding the protection enjoyed by formal workers.

Similar evidences are also available from a number of studies considering the condition of the informal sector in other developing countries. The evidence and the line of reasoning presented above may actually find stronger validation from some of these articles. Alleyne (2001), for example, looks at the case of Jamaica, which mirrors a similar image with respect to labour market outcomes. There has been considerable informalization of the labour market as the pool of self-employed, contract workers, contractors and generally lower level workers have grown.[11] Due to a rise in formal labour costs, employers are opting more for part-time and contract workers on less binding labour contracts. There are continuing debates on whether the informal sector is turning into a refuge for unproductive or low-productive workers in the economy.

However, Funkhouser (1994) shows empirically for five Central American countries that there is a dynamic sub-sector within the informal sector. While informal employment is significant in these countries, its magnitude varies

---

[10] 1 crore = 0.01 billion.
[11] Also see Johnson et al. (1997) and Brand et al. (1993) regarding Zimbabwe; Musyoki and Orodho (1993) regarding economic reform and the informal sector in Kenya; Tripp (1997) on Tanzania, and so forth.

inversely with the level of development (also see Saavedra and Chong 1999). There are substantial returns to human capital variables in each country, which makes the sub-sector dynamic. Nevertheless, informal workers are predominantly female and the male–female wage gap is higher in this sector than in the formal sector. More post-reform evidence on informal sector employment shows that there is a tendency for employment growth. Saavedra and Chong (1999) show that economic growth tends to increase participation in the service sector in the economy, which is concerned with activities on which informal sector typically thrives. They also show that differences persist between informal and formal wage earners. Apparently, the informal wage earners may be showing lower returns to education because their work is repetitive and requires low intellectual abilities, thereby leaving little room for education-related differences (Heckman and Sedlacek 1985). In the case of Peru, the workers are young and less skilled, and there is a positive return to experiences. This may be suggestive of the fact that workers in the informal sector are not productive enough to enter the formal sector. Many thus view employment in the informal sector as a transient stage until the productivity of workers increases enough to enable them to apply for formal sector employment.

While all these studies refer specifically to the developing countries, there is also some reported informal activity in the developed countries. For informal sector experiences of the developed countries, one can refer to the articles by Ihrig and Moe (2000), Jepsen (1991) and others. The debate as to whether economic reform contracts or expands the informal sector may be inconclusive, but it can be unambiguously argued that the lifetime loss in the economy's capital stock is minimal in the presence of the informal sector. Even for the United States, it may be efficient to sustain an informal sector wherein about 5 per cent of the time is devoted to generating only about 3 per cent of the GDP in a steady state.

The presence of the large catch-all informal sector can, therefore, substantially alter the nature of the wage-employment problem facing any developing country. There is, in fact, a general concern that large employment expansion in the informal sector will reduce informal wage. However, on the contrary, global evidence broadly suggests that the wages in the informal sector have gone up in most cases instead of falling due to high employment pressure. It has been argued earlier in this article that one of the factors responsible for this apparently puzzling outcome is the high production growth in such sectors aided by a suitable inflow of capital from various sources. For example, the current real estate boom in various parts of India has drawn enormous formal capital and informal labour in the same place.

An important first step in facilitating more such interactions is perhaps due recognition by the state that the informal sector is a fact of life and it might be easier to improve than reverse conditions of existence of workers in this sector. In this connection, one must also realize that the story of the informal sector is not entirely one of antipathy. There are rich pockets within the informal sector that evade payments of direct or indirect taxes by simply maintaining the informal nature of their trade and by settling for handsome bribes with the law enforcement authorities. The uncontrolled expansion of the informal sector has largely been a product of corruption and often, passive acceptance at the state level in the absence of employment-generating formal industries. There should be little doubt that, if, instead, the enormous capacity within the informal sector can be exploited to its own advantage, the greatest beneficiaries would be the poorest section of the labour force both in terms of living and working conditions.

Saibal Kar, Centre for Studies in Social Sciences, Calcutta, India. E-mail: saibal@cssscal.org

References

Aghion, Philippe, Robin Burgess, Stephen Redding and Fabrizio Zilibotti. 2005. *The Unequal Effects of Liberalization: Evidence from Dismantling the License Raj in India*. Unpublished.

Alleyne, Dillon. 2001. 'The Dynamics of Growth, Employment and Economic Reforms in Jamaica', *Social and Economic Studies*, 50(1): 55–125.

Anant, T. C. A. and Omkar Goswami. 1995. 'Getting Everything Wrong: India's Policy Regarding Sick Firms', in Dilip Mukherjee (ed.), *Essays in Industrial Policy*. New Delhi: Oxford University Press.

Annual Survey of Industries (ASI). Various Issues, Ministry of Industry, Government of India.

Besley, Timothy and Robin Burgess. 2004. 'Can Labour Regulation Hinder Economic Performance? Evidence from India', *Quarterly Journal of Economics*, 119(1): 91–134.

Bhalotra, S. 1998. 'The Puzzle of Jobless Growth in Indian Manufacturing', *Oxford Bulletin of Economics and Statistics*, 60(1): 5–32.

Bhattacharjea, A. 2006. 'Labour Market Regulations and Industrial Performance in India: A Critical Review of the Empirical Evidence', *The Indian Journal of Labour Economics*, 49(2): 211–32.

Brand, V. P. Gumbo and R. Mupedziswa. 1993. 'Women Informal Sector Workers and Structural Adjustments in Zimbabwe', in *Social Change and Economic Reform in Africa*. Uppsala: Scandinavian Institute of African Studies.

Chaudhuri, Kaushik, Rupayan Pal and Bibhas Saha. 2006. *Labour Unions and Trade and Industrial Reforms: Evidence from India*. Unpublished.

Dutta Roy, Sudipta. 2003. 'Employment Dynamics in Indian Industry: Adjustment Lags and the Impact of Job Security Regulations', *Journal of Development Economics*, 73(1): 233–56.

Fallon, Peter and Robert Lucas. 1991. 'The Impact of Job Security Regulations in India and Zimbabwe', *The World Bank Economic Review*, 5(3): 395–413.

Fallon, Peter and Robert Lucas. 1993. 'Job Security Regulations and the Dynamic Demand for Labour in India and Zimbabwe', *Journal of Development Economics*, 40(2): 241–75.

Funkhouser, Edward. 1994. 'The Urban Informal Sector in Central America: Household Survey Evidence', Santa Barbara Working Papers in Economics, University of California: 23–94.

Hasan, R., D. Mitra and K. V. Ramaswamy. 2003. 'Trade Reforms, Labour Regulations and Labour–Demand Elasticities: Empirical Evidence from India', Working Paper 9879, National Bureau of Economic Research. Revised version forthcoming in *Review of Economics and Statistics*.

Heckman, J. and G. Sedlacek. 1985. 'Heterogeneity, Aggregation and Market Wage Functions: An Empirical Model of Self-Selection in the Labor Market', *Journal of Political Economy*, 93(6): 1077–1125.

Ihrig, Jane and Karine S. Moe. 1994. 'The Dynamics of Informal Employment', Board of Governors of the Federal Reserve System, International Finance Discussion Paper: 664.

International Labour Organisation (ILO). 1972. *Informal Sector*. Geneva, Switzerland: ILO.

Jepsen, G. 1991. 'Wage Contracts and Design of Tax Enforcement Policy in the Shadow Economy', Working Paper No 21, Aarhus Institute of Economics Memo.

Johnson, Simon, D. Kaufmann and A. Shleifer. 1997. 'The Unofficial Economy in Transition', *Brookings Paper on Economic Activity*, 10(2): 159–221.

Kar, S. and Sugata Marjit. 2001. 'Informal Sector in General Equilibrium: Welfare Effects of Trade Policy Reforms', *International Review of Economics and Finance*, 10(3): 289–300.

Klapper, Leora, Luc Laeven and Raghuram Rajan. 2005. 'Barriers to Entrepreneurship', Working Paper, University of Chicago.

Kurukshetra, A. and Gulab Singh. 1999. 'Gross Domestic Product and Employment in the Informal Sector of the Indian Economy', *Indian Journal of Labour Economics*, 42(2): 217–30.

Lucas, R.E.B. 1988. 'Demand for *India's Manufacturing Exports'*, *Journal of Development Economics*, 29(1): 63–75.

Mahadevia, Darshini. 1996. 'Informalisation of Employment and Incidence of Poverty in Ahmedabad', *Indian Journal of Labour Economics*, 41(3): 515–30.

Marjit, S. and S. Kar. 2007. 'The Urban Informal Sector and Poverty Effects of Trade Reform and Capital Mobility in India', *Poverty and Economic Policy Network, MPIA* Working Paper no. 2007–09.

Ministry of Finance, Government of India. 2006. *Economic Survey* 2005–06.

Mitra, Arup. 1998. 'Employment in the Informal Sector', *Indian Journal of Labour Economics*, 41(3).

———. 2006. 'Wages and Employment: Issues and Facts', *Indian Journal of Labour Economics*, 49(4): 587–602.

Mookherjee, Dilip. 1995. *Indian Industry: Policies and Performance*. New Delhi: Oxford University Press.

Musyoki, A. and J. Orodho. 1993. 'Urban Women Workers in the Informal Sector and Economic Change in Kenya in the 1980s', in *Social Change and Economic Reform in Africa*. Uppsala: Scandinavian Institute of African Studies.

Nagaraj, R. 1994. 'Employment and Wages in Manufacturing Industries: Trends, Hypotheses and Evidence', *Economic and Political Weekly*, 29(4): 177–86.

———. 2007. 'Labour Market in India: Current Concerns and Policy Responses', OECD Paper.

Saavedra, J. and Alberto Chong. 1999. 'Structural Reform, Institutions and Earnings: Evidence from the Formal and Informal Sectors in Urban Peru', *Journal of Development Studies*, 35(4): 95–116.

Saha, Bibhas. 2006. 'Labour Institutions in India and China: A Tale of Two Nations', *Journal of South Asian Development*, 1(2): 179–205.

Sharma, Alakh N. 2006. 'Flexibility, Employment and Labour Market Reforms in India', *Economic and Political Weekly*, 41(21): 2078–85.

Tendulkar, Suresh D. 2004. 'Organised Labour Market in India: Pre and Post Reform'. Paper presented at the Conference on Anti Poverty and Social Policy in India organized by Mac Arthur Research Network on Inequality and Economic Performance at the Neemrana Fort Palace, Alwar, Rajasthan, January 2–4.

The Ministry of Labour, Government of India. *Indian Labour Yearbook*, Various Issues.

Tripp, A.M. 1997. *Changing the Rules: The Politics of Liberalization and the Urban Informal Economy in Tanzania.* Berkeley and London: University of California Press.

Webster, L. and P. Fidler. 1996. *The Informal Sector and Microfinance in West Africa'*. Washington DC: World Bank Regional and Sectoral Studies, World Bank.

World Development Report. 2000. New York: United Nations.

Zagha, Robert. 1998. 'Labour and India's Economic Reforms', *Journal of Policy Reform*, 2(4): 403–26.

Section II

Section II

Macroeconomics and Sustainable Accounting of Resources and Income

RAMPRASAD SENGUPTA[*]
Centre for Economic Studies and Planning, School of Social Sciences, Jawaharlal Nehru University

SHALINI SAKSENA[*]
Delhi College of Arts and Commerce, University of Delhi

This article focuses on the conceptual and methodological issues relating to the sustainable accounting of income and wealth with illustrative examples in the macroeconomic context. The key macroeconomic performance indicators like Gross Domestic Product (GDP) and Net Domestic Product (NDP) and other aggregates, on which the Standard National Accounts (SNA) of UN focus, have their conceptual basis on the short-run Keynesian macroeconomic models and not on any long-run growth theory. The conventional SNA definition and its coverage of National Accounts do not, in fact, take account of the environmental consequences of economic activities and their feedback impact on their sustainability. This article provides the rationale for enlargement of the scope and coverage of National Accounts of income and wealth so as to include the natural resource (asset) accounting as a component in it as following from the very concept of sustainable development.

The article further shows with illustration how the physical and hybrid flow accounts which would depict the environment–economy interaction along with the material balances can be developed by using the input-output modelling framework of analysis. It finally derives from such accounts the environmentally adjusted indicators of macroeconomic development like GDP, NDP, savings, and so forth, and points to the usefulness of the integration of environmental and economic accounting for the development of sustainable development policies. It describes the satellite System of Environmental-Economic Accounting (SEEA) of the UN for such integration of accounts, and reviews the state of its implementation in India.

JEL Classification: Q56, Q01, E01, E19
Keywords: Sustainable development, Natural Resource Accounting (NRA), System of Integrated Environmental and Economic Accounts (SEEA), Environmental input-output modelling, India

[*] The authors would like to thank Prof. Sugata Marjit for his useful comments and suggestions on the draft version of this article.

1. Introduction

As the level of human well-being of the people of a society is dependent on the material consumption of the produced goods and services, the conventional macroeconomics has focused on the growth and fluctuation of gross domestic production, national income, and its constituent expenditure categories along with employment and prices. Macroeconomic policies have broadly targeted economic growth, full employment, balance of payments equilibrium and price stability. The national income accounts were devised in the 1930s to provide measures of aggregate social production, income and various expenditure components (consumption, investment, net trade, and so forth) so that their changes from year to year could be observed through these statistics, and the performance of the macroeconomy could be monitored and analyzed. Such national accounts have evolved under the framework of the Standard National Accounts (SNA) of the United Nations (UN) in different countries to measure the Gross Domestic Product (GDP) and the Net National Product (NNP), among many other related aggregates. However, such accounts have conventionally delimited the scope and coverage of income to such domains of production for which the products as well as the factor inputs are transacted in the market or their uses have clear opportunity price or cost in terms of some market prices. While the consumers of an economy dictate the goods and services to be produced and transacted in the market, and the market works efficiently under competitive conditions to allocate resources, stimulate production and enhance the quantity, quality and diversity of goods and services made available to the consumers, there are domains of production and natural resource use wherein the market fails to work efficiently. The national accounts based on market transaction and prices have, in fact, been considered unsatisfactory as a measure of true income or as indicators of long-term sustainable growth or welfare for the following reasons of limitations of the market:

(*i*) The scope of production does not include own consumption of certain goods and services which are produced by households but not transacted in the market. In most cases, the own factor services, which are used in production, are also left out in aggregate income estimates. The examples are those of household labour time used for firewood collection or bringing water, looking after children, and so forth.

(*ii*) The public good character of the ecological services of resource generation and waste absorption rendered by the natural environment does not often permit the market to function, nor does it provide any price signal for these services.

As the property rights cannot often be defined on the concerned natural resource base, the conventional national accounts system, as developed under the SNA framework before 1993, had not accounted for the values of such pure ecological functions of nature which provide crucial support to the economic system as a source for the natural resource inputs and as a sink for the absorption of the wastes. A serious implication of this neglect of the concern for scarcity of the in-place environmental resources (that is, resources in an undeveloped and unmanaged condition, like coal in steam, standing timber, and so forth) is that, these have often been implicitly treated as free goods. This neglect has also implied that nature has an indefinitely large capacity of waste absorption, which is far from the reality in the present state of the natural environment in both industrialized and developing countries. The NDP or the National Income, as currently estimated, cannot thus be interpreted as an indicator of sustainable well-being at the macroeconomic level as it is likely to be an overestimate of the true income or equivalently the sustainable level of well-being.

The discussion in this article is confined to the conceptual issues relating to sustainable accounting in the macroeconomic context. This would essentially involve the introduction of natural resource accounting and the enlargement of the scope and coverage of the national accounts of income and wealth with some structural changes. The motivation behind such environmental adjustment of accounts would be to capture the environmental consequences of the economic activities of production and consumption in both physical and value terms in the estimation of growth of assets and of sustainable or true income. In this context, the theoretical rationale and the basis of such environmental accounting are outlined and the integration of the economic and the environmental accounting as has been proposed by the UN (UNSD 1993) under the framework of a satellite System of Environmental-Economic Accounting (SEEA), is described. In this context, conceptual issues and problem of measurement and valuation of the natural assets due to both their depletion and qualitative degradation are also discussed. The description of the integration of environmental and economic accounting would focus on the framework of such accounts to reflect the environmental consequences of the economic activity through illustration as they are expected to follow from our analytical models. The approach of development of integrated accounts in some selected countries and its state of development in India are also referred to at places in this article.

2. Neo-classical Economics and the Natural Environment

It may be noted at this stage that the environmental economists mostly belonging to the neo-classical school have since long been treating the effects of production and consumption on the environment as those of externalities. The problems of over-use of natural common resources or under-provision of public goods like environmental protection involving cost sharing have been considered by them as ones arising from ill-defined property rights, the public good character of environmental products, and market failure. They have developed and analyzed a wide variety of policy issues relating to environmental protection and natural resource conservation, which essentially involved the use of ideas, principles and tools of welfare economics, public economics, public finance and institutional economics. The use of shadow prices of environmental resources, environmental cost-benefit analysis, the design of tax subsidies or other instruments of quantitative control, and the development of participatory institutions for common resource management, and so forth, have, for example, addressed a wide range of environmental issues. A rich literature of environmental and resource economics has developed as a result of extensive research in the area over the last three to four decades. While making such applications of principles of neo-classical economics in the context of the use and protection of natural environmental resources, the environmental and resource economists realized the necessity of both an assessment of the physical environmental impact of economic processes using methods of science and technology, and at the same time, that of development of methods of monetary valuation of environmental benefits or damages. The need for inventorization and evaluation of environmental impacts would arise in any situation wherein social costs differ from private costs on account of market failure. Although such impact assessment and valuation of nature have been important for evaluating development projects and environmental policy, would it warrant a change of the macroeconomic accounting system for the purpose of correct policies? One may, in fact, argue that any mis-allocation of resources due to divergence between the social cost and the private cost of economic processes arising from environmental externalities can be corrected through appropriate public policy intervention and/or the development of new institutions. This should not, therefore, necessitate a change of the accounting system, the yardstick of measurement of change or the progress itself. If the purpose is the greening of the economy, it can be done without changing the accounting system. Why do we need greening of the accounting system itself?

3. Macroeconomic Accounting and the Natural Environment

The problem, however, arises at the macroeconomic level with the conventional accounting system for a different reason. The national accounts provide the measures of success or failure of the major macroeconomic objective, that is, economic growth. Income accounting measures like GDP or NDP and their constituents, by expenditure or factor income categories, provide essential data for the economic analysis of macroeconomic performance or for future development planning. They are important not only as measures of changes in the level of economic activities, but also as values of the tools for economic stabilization, resource mobilization and short- and medium-run demand side management policies. While the conceptual basis of the rules of aggregation of values to obtain the estimates of macroeconomic variables of the national accounts has been the neo-classical market theory, the key indicators on which the SNA focuses are based mostly on the short-run Keynesian macro-models and not on any long-run growth theory or models. As a result, it is not surprising that the scope and coverage of national accounts is considered to be inadequate for obtaining information on the determinants of the process of growth and sustainability of development.

It may be noted here that the national accounts of many countries like India have only flow accounts of production, income and expenditure, but no accounts of economic assets which would include non-produced economic assets like land, sub-soil minerals, fossil fuel resources, and so forth. As a result, the national accounts cannot generate adequate statistics on the tools of long-run growth affecting sustainability. Nor are such accounts based on any long-run theory of growth and sustainability. The Hicksian definition of income describes income to be the maximum sustainable long-term constant consumption over time (Hicks 1946). The conventional SNA definition of income allows for adjustment of the gross value added for the depreciation of man-made capital but not for the depreciation of natural capital and, therefore, does not represent a truly Hicksian income. The measures of income and investment of such accounts, as they are estimated, are thus imperfect indicators of the level of human well-being, the sustainability of which is a major macroeconomic goal in the long run.

Given the method of estimating aggregate income and asset accumulation as arising mostly from economic activities involving market transactions, the consequences of environment–economy interaction, which have a significant bearing on the sustainability of economic processes, are not reflected in the national accounts. A change in the national asset and national income accounting system is required so as to ensure that the environmental consequences of development activities or the effects of environmental policies on the macroeconomy are adequately reflected in the data of the accounts and the latter can provide statistics on the indicators and tools of sustainable development. A change in the yardstick of measurement of economic change or progress, as would be given by the change in the accounting system, would change the policy priority as well. Ideally, what is desired is that the scope of coverage of asset and production-cum-income national accounts should be broadened enough with appropriate re-classification of the items of income and expenditure so as to serve the macro-economic policy goals of short-run stabilization and full employment, and long-run growth and sustainability. In view of these concerns, the framework of the SNA as developed in the UNSD, 1993 (hereafter referred to as the SNA 1993) and the follow-up development of the operational manual of the SEEA have kept the earlier market-based production, income and expenditure accounts giving the core macroeconomic identities as unchanged. The new accounting framework prescribes the development of a satellite system of economy environment accounts which would consist of several interactive modules covering the different aspects of interaction. The World Bank has independently developed conceptual papers and estimates of true/ sustainable income with adjustments for not only man-made capital but also natural capital (see Hamilton and Clemens 1999; Hamilton and Ruta 2006; World Bank 2006, and so forth).

The satellite system would cover the flow accounts of the supply and use of product, income, resources and wastes along with environmental protection expenditure (maintenance cost of emissions). The system also covers physical and monetary accounts of all produced and non-produced economic assets, man-made and natural, and those of non-produced environmental assets (as explained later). These accounts would reflect changes in the stocks of various types of assets due to investment, natural growth, depreciation of produced assets, and depletion and degradation of non-produced natural assets on account of economic activities, ecological functions and other reasons. The satellite system also shows the overall integration of the economic and environmental accounts pointing to the linkages between stocks and flows of asset and income, and arriving at the estimates of the true costs, sustainable income, and genuine savings and investment. In other words, the satellite accounts system should be able to tell us about the consequences, both of economic activities on the environment and of environmental policy measures for protection on economic transactions.

The worldwide economic growth and growth of the population since the middle of the twentieth century have caused increasing pressure on the environmental and natural resource base of the different economies. It is now widely recognized that the circular flow of income of elementary macroeconomics can be maintained in the set-up of such growing economies only by increasingly intensive use of natural resources and land, and growing volume of pollution. Ecological economists like Daly and Farley (2003) have addressed the issue of sustainability as one of a development process which recognizes the limits of scale of flow of throughput from nature to the human system and characterizes it to be representative of qualitative and not quantitative changes of human society and economy. Such changes are supposed to be brought out by way of the development of technology, knowledge, institutional innovations and structural adjustments, and thereby a realization of its full potential. They have, therefore, raised the issue of optimum scale of economic activity and visualized development as an evolution of the economy and society to represent an improved (and not necessarily larger) structure or system. In the environmental macroeconomics, the discussion has, however, centred not on the short-run issues relating to the stabilization of demand, employment, output and wage prices, but on how economic growth, structural changes and changes in the pattern of trade would affect the environment. Similarly, the discussions also address the issues relating to the effects of environmental and energy policies on the developments of technology, production and trade. The capital theoretic macroeconomic models of optimal growth, on the other hand, have analyzed the conditions of sustainability in terms of its relation with the environmental resource base and its composition, by broadening the notion of capital to include natural capital. As shall be seen in the following section, a sustainable accounting system of national income and natural resources would have its theoretical basis on such models. The Integrated Environmental and Economic Accounting, on the other hand, as shall be seen, has its basis in the multi-sector linear models of general equilibrium. Such an integrated accounting system would, in fact, offer opportunities of the development of macro level multi-sector computing policy models for long-run sustainable development.

4. Economy–Environment Interaction and National Income Accounting

Economic activity involves two-way interactions between nature and economy. The production of goods and services requires flow of material resources as well as other environmental services for the conversion of the former into products, which are either consumed or directly or indirectly used in the production system in an entropic matter. The wastes, which arise at the end of the life-cycle of material resources, flow back to the natural environment which provides a sink service for the absorption of the wastes. The solar energy flow and the bio-geo-chemical cycles enable nature to degrade these wastes and regenerate resources. However, since nature provides the supply of such an environmental service of resource regeneration and waste absorption at a fixed rate, there is a maximum rate of primary productivity of low entropy resources and a maximum rate of depreciation of polluting high entropy wastes per unit of time. If the economic activities were organized in such a way that the rate of resource use exceeds the limits of resource supply, and if the rate of waste generation exceeds the capacity level of waste absorption, the stock of natural resources would be depleted without replenishment and the unabsorbed wastes would accumulate as pollutant stock in the environment. Such polluting stocks would degrade the environment, while the overuse of resources would lead to a situation of resource scarcity. The growing pollution would generate adverse externalities causing health injuries to humans and adversely affecting the primary productivity of the natural ecosystems.

The conventional national accounts do not provide any deduction for depletion and degradation of the in-place natural resource stock for finding out the estimate of NDP, while they allow for the deduction on account of the depreciation of the man-made capital. If man-made capital had been the only type of capital which is scarce in availability, then the conventional NDP would have ensured sustainability of consumption at some constant level over time, and we need not have bothered about the environmental adjustment of concepts and measures. In view of the growing scarcity of natural capital, the applicability of the Hicksian concept in National Income Accounting would require an explicit recognition of the use of the different types of environmental services and their valuation so that the accounts may reflect the depletion and degradation of the environmental assets, and indicate the estimates of true income in the Hicksian sense and the true measure of net wealth formation.

The notion of sustainability of the development process as conceived by the World Commission on Environment and Development is based on an ethical theory of inter-generational equity. A capital theoretic framework of the analysis of sustainable development as developed in the literature (Dasgupta and Mäler 2000; Dasgupta 2001; Dasgupta and Mitra 2001; Mäler, 1991; Hartwick 1977; Weitzman 1976) quite sharply points to the need for resource accounting as an essential condition for implementing any policy of sustainable development. This point is elaborated to emphasize the inter-dependence of different components of the stock of total capital of a nation and the importance of their accounting in determining the sustainability of the growth process.

5. A Model of Sustainable Development

The ethical theory of inter-generational equity, first of all, implies that the well-being of a society is to be defined not as *current* social well-being, but as social well-being *over time*. Let the social well-being over time be represented by the discounted present equivalent of the inter-temporal profile of instantaneous utilities which depend on consumption. A Ramsey–Koopmans type inter-temporal social utility function, defined over an infinite time horizon, is used for an economy with stationary population as follows:

$$V(\tau) = \int_{\tau}^{\infty} u\{c(t)\}e^{-r(t-\tau)}dt \tag{1}$$

where t is the time, c the consumption of goods and services, r the time rate of discount, and $u\{c(t)\}$ the current utility out of consumption in period t.

The aggregate social product (GDP or Y) of our economy may be conceived as a composite good which can be used for consumption $c(t)$, investment in man-made capital assets $k(t)$ and spending on environmental pollution abatement $z(t)$. Here, a simplifying assumption is made that the man-made and the natural capital are the only scarce resources in the economy in order to focus on the relevance of asset and resource accounting in the national accounts. The GDP is produced by using the services of man-made capital $\{k(t)\}$, which is subject to depreciation, and drawing upon the flow resources $\{R(t)\}$ from the stock of natural capital $\{N(t)\}$, which is regenerated by nature. The factor productivities are, however, affected by the stock of pollutants $\{P(t)\}$ in the environment due to externalities.

The stock of pollutants, on the other hand, is the unabsorbed residual of emission flow arising from production and deposited in nature. This stock is degraded by the bio-geo-chemical cycles of nature as driven by the solar energy flow. The dynamics of these resource stocks may be represented formally as follows:

s.t $\quad \dot{k}(t) = f\{k(t), R(t), (P(t)\} - c(t) - z(t) - \delta k(t)$ \hfill (2)

$\quad \dot{N}(t) = \phi\{N(t), P(t)\} - R(t)$ \hfill (3)

$\quad \dot{P}(t) = G\{R(t), z(t)\} - \theta P(t)$ \hfill (4)

$\quad k(\tau), N(\tau)$ and $P(\tau)$ being given

where f is the production function of the gross social product,
ϕ is the regeneration function of resources by nature,
and G is the function representing pollution arising from the use of the natural resource throughput and spending on pollution abatement.
δ and θ are the rates of depreciation of man-made capital and that of the degradation of pollutant stock per period by natural cycles.

It may be noted here that $f_k \geq 0, f_R \geq 0, f_P < 0$;

$\phi_N > 0, \ \phi_P > 0, \ G_R > 0$ and $G_Z < 0$ in the relevant domain of values of the concerned variables.

The dynamics of the various stocks, whose initial values are given, would yield an inter-temporal utility profile as determined by the Resource Allocation Mechanism (RAM) of the society which is defined by the institutional arrangements of production and distribution. This allocation mechanism may not be perfect from the viewpoint of either competitiveness or that of attaining the first best social optimum (Dasgupta 2001). The present equivalent value of the utility profile or the measure of social well-being over time thus generated by the RAM would, in fact, be equivalent to the aggregate value of all the capital stocks using the prices which are derived from the marginal value productivities of the different types of capital stocks over time. A given initial configuration of $K(\tau)$, $N(\tau)$ and $P(\tau)$, and the resource allocation mechanism, say α, would yield a time path of the variables $\{c(t), R(t), z(t), k(t), N(t), P(t)\}_\alpha$ and correspondingly a utility profile $[u\{c(t)\}]_\alpha$ and a value of $V_\tau(\alpha)$. The shadow rentals for the use of the stocks as arising from the process would yield the initial stock prices at the time τ as the discounted initial equivalent value. The aggregate value of these initial capital stocks as per such prices would be $V_\tau(\alpha)$. The sustainability of the development process would thus mean that the social well-being over time, or equivalently, the aggregate value of all the stocks of resources or wealth of the society, should be non-declining with the passage of time.

The sustainability condition would then imply:

$$
\frac{dV^*(\tau)}{d(\tau)} = \frac{\partial V^*(\tau)}{\partial k(\tau)} \cdot \frac{dk(\tau)}{d\tau} + \frac{\partial V^*(\tau)}{\partial N(\tau)} \cdot \frac{dN(\tau)}{d\tau} + \frac{\partial V^*(\tau)}{\partial P(\tau)} \cdot \frac{dP(\tau)}{d\tau}
$$

$$
= p(\tau)\frac{dk}{d\tau} + \pi(\tau)\frac{dN}{d\tau} + \mu(\tau)\frac{dP}{d\tau}
$$

$$
= I_k(\tau) + I_N(\tau) + I_P(\tau)
$$

$$
= I(\tau) \geq 0 \tag{5}
$$

for all values of τ as we move along the time scale where $V^*(\tau)$ is the attainable value of $V(\tau)$ under the RAM; $p(\tau)$, $\pi(\tau)$ and $\mu(\tau)$ are the respective stock prices and where I_k, I_N and I_P are the respective investment values in man-made capital, natural capital and pollution stock. I is the aggregate true investment. The sustainability of development thus requires that true investment, which is the aggregate value of investments in all kinds of capital assets of a society, should be non-negative.

The composition of this investment thus needs to be examined for understanding its precise implication in respect of natural resource accounting and the sustainability character of the development process needs to be empirically tested. One important implication of the condition (5) of the above model is that the society's genuine or true measure of investment or accumulation of wealth, which would contribute to the progress of well-being, is not just the value of net accumulation of man-made capital, but the total value of net accumulation of man-made capital, natural capital and pollution stock, the last one being the accumulation of a public bad. If there is an over-harvesting of the resources of nature, which exceeds the limit of nature's ability to regenerate resources and if the gross emission of pollutants, in spite of abatement expenditure, exceeds the ecosystem's ability to absorb, then $N(\tau)>0$ and $P(\tau)>0$ leading to $I_N < 0$ and $I_P < 0$, since $\pi(\tau)$ and $\mu(\tau)$ are expected to be positive and negative values, respectively. This would imply that $I_E = I_N + I_P < 0$ where I_E gives the aggregate measure of depletion of the environmental resource base of the economy, which includes the entire array of natural resources—fossil fuels, minerals, land and soil, water, forest and other vegetation and abiotic resources, atmosphere, ocean, lakes, rivers, and so forth. While the basic elemental contents of matter and energy of all these natural resource assets remain unchanged over time, the time rate of their human use often tends to exceed the scale of intervention that nature can withstand, resulting in the dissipation of resources due to the entropy laws.

6. Resource and Environmental Accounting

In order to assess the performance of a macroeconomy and its state of the environment in the context of sustainability, it is therefore,primarily important to extend and adjust the scope and structure of the asset or wealth account of an economy by incorporating the consequences of the economy–environment interaction in terms of net resource depletion or degradation from year to year. The natural resource accounting thus becomes crucial to monitor and understand the character of the environmental impact of the economic processes on the assets and to derive policy implications. While one may similarly argue for the relevance of accounting for human capital formation and for the adjustment of national accounts to the extent that non-market factors play a role in human skill formation, those issues will not be dwelt on in this article, which will focus on the sustainable accounting for I_N and I_P.

As the neo-classical production function allows substitutability between natural capital and man-made capital in our model, the sustainability of social well-being (in a weak sense) over time may be attainable by moderating the demand for the withdrawal of resources $R(t)$ from the stock of natural resources $N(t)$, or by reducing the occurrence of gross pollution. This can be achieved by investing in energy and material resource-conserving technologies. This would be reflected in the substitution of $R(t)$ by $K(t)$. This would also have a beneficial effect on rising pollution because of the relation of material balance between the material resource flow and the return waste flow as per the entropy law. The composition of the capital stock and the dynamics of their change thus need to be explicitly monitored and analyzed for guiding the policies and actions for sustainable development. Resource accounting is supposed to monitor these values in physical and monetary terms.

While the macroeconomic production function, as assumed in our conceptual model, permits substitutability between man-made and natural capital, the strong sustainability consideration emphasizes that the environmental resource stocks should be maintained and protected from both net quantitative depletion and qualitative degradation. This may necessitate appropriate spending on current or capital account for the discovery of new resources or the upgradation of the existing resources or development of backstop resource and technology. Examples can be given of investment for the discovery of new oil deposits, or alternative energy resources, change in land use, forest development and management for promoting biotic growth or culture of biological resources, and so forth.

Similarly, the spending on pollution abatement technologies on both current account and capital account would contribute to the reduction of pollution or to the cleaning up of the environment—particularly air, water bodies and land—and to the conservation of the resource regenerating ability of the ecosystem.

Part of this spending on the primary and intermediate inputs for resource development or pollution abatement would be reflected in the changes in the man-made capital assets in the form of fixed non-residential or other structures and equipments, for example, rigs for oil exploration or pollution abatement equipments, in the macro asset account.

The remaining part of the spending would be mainly reflected in the asset account as changes in the developed natural assets (or what may alternatively be called non-produced economic assets) which have been obtained by way of transfer of resources from the natural environment where they were lying in an undeveloped state, to the economic environment, in order to make them suitable for utilization in economic activities. These changes should be reflected in most of the cases in both the physical and monetary values of the concerned resources, for example, developed sub-soil assets, changes in land use, and so forth. Some of these spendings may result in only qualitative changes like upgrading water quality or air quality indicators in terms of concentration of the pollutants in the concerned water body, air shed, and so forth, which may not be easily estimated in value terms because of the immediate non-marketability of the benefits. These values of developed or protected natural assets, whenever estimable, would, in fact, contain the scarcity value of the undeveloped *in situ* resource or the natural environment as well as the costs of consumption of fixed capital assets and other primary and intermediate inputs, which were used for this transfer or protection, and which contributed to the augmentation of utilizable $N(t)$ or to the abatement of $P(t)$.

In any case, it is clear that the replenishment of the physical levels of depleted natural resource stock or the abatement of the pollutant stock would often raise the volume of economic activities and GDP and also the gross value of capitalized assets or gross investment vis-à-vis a situation of neglect of environmental consideration in accounting. However, if such spending replenishes the depleted environmental stock, such additions of values to GDP or Gross Investment would offset the depreciation of natural assets, which were induced by the economic activities. The investment for replenishment or maintenance of such environmental resources should, therefore, be deducted when we have to work out the NDP or true investment. In fact, if in an economy, the actual replenishment or restoration of environmental assets is not adequate, the entire natural capital depreciation is to be provided for, for deriving the estimates of Hicksian income as well as the true investment for an economy.

One important fallout of the above discussion on the conceptual theory of the sustainability of economic processes and its practical implication is the recognition of the need for the following changes in our macroeconomic accounting system:

(*a*) To measure the opening physical resource stocks, their monetary values, and their changes with the compositional break-up during the concerned period, which are relevant to the sustainability of economic processes.

(*b*) To restructure the wealth asset account of the economy in order to take account of natural resource accounting in (*a*), and showing the linkage between man-made fixed capital with environmental resource development and protection.

(*c*) To adjust the Production, Income and Expenditure accounts of the economy in order to take account of resource accounting and make it consistent with the changes in the wealth account in order to generate the estimates of true income NDP at the macro level. The details of the re-oriented account should clarify the role of environment in production.

7. Sustainability Benchmarks for Adjustment of Macroeconomic Aggregates

Before we proceed for further details of resource accounting or the adjustment of national accounts of income and wealth, it is important to remove certain confusions in the context of the environmental adjustment of wealth and income estimates. It is often argued, for example, that since environmental protection expenditure or resource development spending are already reflected in the transactions of the economy to the extent that they actually take place, it is not clear why there should arise any need for adjustment on their account, or how precisely such adjustments should be done. Should we deduct the entire value of a sub-soil natural resource as sold in the market from the GDP to obtain sustainable NDP? Alternatively, should the entire spending for pollution abatement or for the discovery of resources to replenish the depleted or degraded stock, undertaken by the business sector, household or government, be subtracted to get net income?

Besides, it is also a common phenomenon that the environmental resource protection measures undertaken during a given period are inadequate for maintaining the environmental resource capacity. It is very often seen that the natural environmental resource base and its capacity have been depleted over a long time, due to neglect. It is often not only a question of replenishing the environmental resource stock as it depreciates during a given year or period in order to maintain the level on a year-to-year basis, as at the beginning of the period, but to restore the capacity to a benchmark level which corresponds to the environmental capacity during the base year period, and is considered normative for the sustainability of the functions of ecosystems (see chapter 1 of SEEA in UNSD 2000). For example, the Kyoto Protocol targets to control the greenhouse gas emission flow to a level marginally lower than that of 1990 levels for the protocol signatory nations. The sustainable capacity requirement would warrant investments to restore the capacity to the benchmark level. The question arises as to how such depletion and degradation of the past and the current period would be treated in the adjustments of wealth or income accounts.

We may, in fact, focus on the latter issue by decomposing the historical loss of environmental capacity as occurring over time to get the norms for environmental adjustment of wealth and income in order to take care of the environmental capacity variation (UNSD 2003).

Let EK_S, EK_T^0, EK_{T0}, EK_{T-1} be explained as follows:

EK_S = Environmental capacity as per the norms of sustainability of functions of an ecosystem.

EK_T^0 = Environmental capacity which would have been attained at the end of period T, in case, there had been no environmental protection activities in the past and the current T^{th} period.

EK_{T0} = Environmental capacity which would have been attained at the end of the Tth period if there had been no environmental protection activities in the Tth period only.

EK_T, EK_{T-1} = Actual environmental capacity attained at the end of the Tth and $T-1^{th}$ period as per the actual development path, which included some measures of environmental protection in the present and the past.

Thus, we may express the following:

ΔEK_1 = Actual protection of environmental capacity in the past and the present period

$= EK_T - EK_T^0$

ΔEK_{1T} = Actual environmental protection as provided in the current period T

$= EK_T - EK_{T0}$

ΔEK_2 = Actual depletion and degradation (emissions) from the economic activities as observed in the Tth period

$= EK_{T-1} - EK_T$

ΔEK_3 = Actual depletion and degradation (emissions) from the past activities till the $T-1^{th}$ period

$= EK_S - EK_{T-1}$

Thus, the gross environmental impact of economic activities before netting out for any protection measure, that is, $EK_S - EK_T^0$, can be decomposed as follows:

$$EK_S - EK_T^0 = \Delta EK_1 + \Delta EK_2 + \Delta EK_3 \tag{6}$$

While ΔEK_1 measures the cumulating estimate of environmental protection, ΔEK_2 and ΔEK_3 measure the estimates of the environmental capacity loss in the present and in the past, respectively. Out of ΔEK_1, ΔEK_{1T} represents the extent of protection that has been provided by spending during the current period T.

Environmental accounting would thus require the proper assessment of EK_T and EK_{T-1} both in physical and monetary value terms. As the income and production account of an economy will show the expenditure for ΔEK_{1T}, but not ΔEK_2 or any share of ΔEK_3, sustainable accounting will require the adjustment of gross income not only for ΔEK_{1T} but also for ΔEK_2, and the share of restoration of environmental capacity to the level ΔEK_S, that is, a share as per some restoration plan as spread over years. See Figure 1.

The theoretical model for the integration of environmental accounting with that of national accounts used to address more precisely the issues raised

FIGURE 1

State of environmental capacity and protection

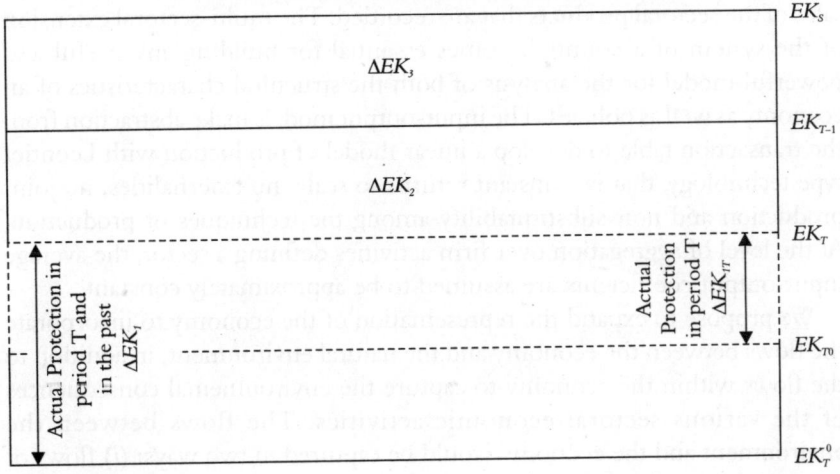

Source: Prepared by the authors.

in the preceding sections however, needs to be disaggregative in order to show the interdependence among the different types of activities according to the nature of their effects on environmental capacity variation and the use of different types of goods and services. An extension of the input-output model as presented in the following section to incorporate the environment–economy interaction would be useful not only to understand the environmental consequences of economic activities and those of environmental protection or resource conservation on the sustainability of economic system, but also to derive the equations or formulae for the environmental adjustments for the macro aggregates and accounts.

8. An Environmental Input-Output Framework of Analysis

The transaction table of an economy shows the inter-sectoral flows and various final uses of goods and services produced in an economy. It also shows the use of various inputs—intermediate and primary—in production in the various sectors of an economy. It is essentially an extension of the national accounts and is central to understanding the inter-sectoral dependence and the role of relative input or resource intensities in determining the structural characteristics of an economy. In the conventional national income accounts, the inter-industrial transactions are netted out and it is only the value added by the different sectors and the value of final sales of the sectoral products that are recorded. The multi-sectoral extension of the system of accounts becomes essential for building any useful and powerful model for the analysis of both the structural characteristics of an economy as well as policies. The input-output models make abstraction from the transaction table to develop a linear model of production with Leontief type technology, that is, constant returns to scale, no externalities, no joint production and non-substitutability among the techniques of production. At the level of aggregation over firm activities defining a sector, the average input-output coefficients are assumed to be approximately constant.

We propose to expand the representation of the economy to incorporate the flows between the economy and the natural environment, in addition to the flows within the economy to capture the environmental consequences of the various sectoral economic activities. The flows between the environment and the economy would be captured in two ways: (*i*) flows of natural resources from the nature to economic activities, and (*ii*) flows of waste arising from the economic activities of production as well as final use, to the natural environmental for their possible absorption (Leontief 1970; Ayres 1978; Pearson 1989; and Perman et al. 1996). Both these types of flows can be conceived as input flows. The natural resources are obviously throughput to the economic system for either material processing for conversion into products or for providing energy or other services for such conversion. While the waste arisings, unless immediately degraded, are by-products with negative use value or external effects, the waste flows may be interpreted as the input use of the sink service of the natural environment to receive the waste flows in order to degrade or store. We do, however, account for the fact that the production system contains waste or pollution abatement activities, which are external to the other different sectors defined, and reduce the pollution by treatment of wastewater, solid waste management, waste treatment, and so forth. The products of such activities may be called environmental protection products, which would also use various types of resources. There are also some abatement measures that are internal to an industrial sector and are built into the basic technology of the concerned production activities. The waste arising from a sector, as defined, would obviously be the net product of such internal abatement.

In the extended framework of environmental input-output analysis, we can thus classify the input flows into four categories:

(*i*) Intermediate inputs of produced goods and services,
(*ii*) Primary inputs of labour and capital,

(*iii*)   Natural resource inputs and

(*iv*)   Waste-flow disposal service of the natural environment.

The producing sectors of the economy can be essentially classified into the following three categories:

(*i*)   Natural resource development and extraction activities like coal mining, iron ore mining, oil extraction, and so forth. It is, in fact, the products of these activities that are used by the other economic sectors. For example, the coal or oil, as produced, would thus for example, be classified in the form of intermediate goods, while the natural resource of coal, as embodied in coal seams or crude oil *in situ* should be considered as inputs in the extraction activities as supplied by nature,

(*ii*)   Environmental protection activities, which abate pollution arisings and

(*iii*)   Other industrial activities.

We shall, however, club (*i*) and (*iii*) together since a number of sectoral activities vertically combine the development of the natural resource with the use of energy, labour and capital, the harvesting of the resource and its processing as is the case in the agriculture, forestry, and fishery sectors. These would, for example, include working on land and soil, forest biomass and biomass of fish stock, and so forth, along with the activities of their development for yielding the sectoral marketed products of agricultural crops, forest and aqua-cultural products.

Let $X=(X_j)$ be the vector of output of sectoral activities other than environmental protection. Let X_{ij}^1 denote the flow of sectoral production from the ith sector for intermediate input use in the jth conventional industrial sector (that is, other than environmental protection industries) and F_i denote its supply to the final user of the product.

Let Y_{kj}^1 be the use of the kth primary factors like labour, man-made capital, and so forth, in the jth conventional industrial sector.

Let R_{lj}^1 and W_{sj}^1 be the flow of the lth natural capital resource to the jth industrial sector and that of sth residual waste from the jth industrial sector to the natural environment, respectively.

Let $Z=(Z_s)$ be the vector of pollution abatement or environmental protection activities. Let X_{im}^2, Y_{km}^2, R_{lm}^2 and W_{sm}^2 be the flows of ith industrial good, k^{th} primary factor service, l^{th} natural resource and s^{th} residual flows of waste to or from the mth environmental protection sector. Let W_s^f be the sth waste flow from the final use of the goods and services F_i for all i together. Let $\overline{W}_s$ be the unabated amount of sth waste flow in the concerned period.

The transaction flows of different products and input flows of the economy are shown in Table 1. Each row of the table shows the flows of products or inputs or wastes to different using sectors. It may be noted that the total gross waste flows would be the total output of the abatement of the concerned waste plus the actual unabated amount. The columns of Table 1, on the other hand, show the spending by the different using sectors in real terms on different inputs including the sink service of nature to obtain the output of the concerned producing sector or the benefit of final use.

TABLE 1

Transaction flows

Users→ Products or inputs↓	Industries other than environmental protection(j)	Environmental protection or pollution abatement sectors (m)	Final users	Total
Industrial products other than environmental protection ones	X_{lj}^1	X_{lm}^2	F_i	X_i
Wastes	W_{sj}^1	W_{sm}^2	W_s^f	$Z_s + \overline{W}_s$
Primary factors	Y_{kj}^1	Y_{km}^2		b_k
Natural capital	R_{lj}^1	R_{lm}^2		r_l

Source: Prepared by the authors.

If now p_i, t_s, v_k, π_l be the prices of the industrial product i, environmental protection product of abating s^{th} waste, primary factor k and natural resource l, we can easily derive a transaction table in value terms for our economy. However, given the assumption of linear technology of Leontief type, we may derive the following input-output model based on Table 1. As far as the flows between the natural environment and the economy are concerned, the nature as a resource supplier is supplying r_l's and receiving as sink $\overline{W}_s$, the unabated net waste. The entropy law and material balance condition would ensure the relationship

$$\theta(r) = \theta_1(\overline{W}) + \theta_2$$

where θ is the total molecular weight of all natural resource throughput represented by the vector r = (r_l),
θ_1 is the total molecular weight of all unabated wastes represented by the vector $\overline{W} = (\overline{W}_s)$. θ_2 is the total molecular weight of all durable material goods

produced and accumulated for future use during the concerned period. θ_2 would depend on the composition of F_i's in terms of consumption, investment, export, and so forth.

For the conventional input-output sectors, the demand–supply balance conditions will yield the condition:

$$X = A_1 X + A_2 Z + F \tag{7}$$

where X, Z and F are the column vectors $X = (X_j)$, $Z = (Z_m)$, $F = (F_i)$.

$A_1 = (a_{ij}^1)$ where $a_{ij}^1 = X_{ij}^1 / X_j$, A_1 is a square matrix.

$A_2 = (a_{im}^2)$ where $a_{im}^2 = X_{im}^2 / Z_m$

For the environmental protection products of waste abatements, the supply–demand balance condition would be

$$Z = W_1 X + W_2 Z + W^f - \overline{W} \tag{8}$$

where matrix $W_1 = \left(w_{sj}^1\right)$ where $w_{sj}^1 = \dfrac{W_{sj}}{X_j}$

$W_2 = \left(w_{sm}^2\right)$ where $w_{sm}^2 = \dfrac{W_{sm}}{Z_m}$ and W_2 is a square matrix.

For the primary factor inputs of labour and man-made capital, and the natural resources, the supply–demand balance conditions would yield the following conditions:

$$b = B_1 X + B_2 Z, \tag{9}$$
$$r = R_1 X + R_2 Z \tag{10}$$

where $b = (b_k)$ and $r = (r_l)$ are the vectors of total primary factor use and natural resource uses, respectively.

$B_1 = \left(b_{kj}^1\right)$ where $b_{kj}^1 = Y_{kj}^1 / X_j$

$B_2 = \left(b_{km}^2\right)$ where $b_{km}^2 = Y_{km}^2 / Z_m$

$R_1 = \left(r_{lj}^1\right)$ where $r_{lj}^1 = R_{lj}^1 / X_j$

$$R_2 = \left(r_{lm}^2 \right) \text{ where } r_{lm}^2 = R_{lm}^2 / Z_m$$

The price-cost condition that will be satisfied under the technological assumptions of the model and the conditions of competition would be as follows:

$$p = pA_1 + vB_1 + \pi R_1 + tW_1 \qquad (11)$$

$$t = pA_2 + vB_2 + \pi R_2 + tW_2 \qquad (12)$$

where $p = (p_i)$, $v = (v_k)$, $\pi = (\pi_l)$, $t = (t_s)$ are the row price vectors of products and inputs.

In this economy, for any given vector of final demand yielding an associated waste arising from final such uses of material goods and given an unabated waste flow level (or net waste flow standard), equations (7) to (10) will solve the gross level of outputs of the conventional industrial sectors and of various waste abatement activities as well as the total uses of primary factors and natural resource inputs. The supportive price system for the industrial goods and pollution abatement services will be solved by equations (11) and (12) for the given primary factor and natural resource prices.

The vectors p and t can be interpreted as marginal costs of production of the conventional industrial products and the marginal costs of abatement of pollution. The final demand F and the demand for environmental standard as indicated by $\overline{W}$ should be consistent with such p and t, and the generated total income as yielded by $vb + \pi r$ if the economy is in equilibrium. The theory of environmental economics would ensure that the marginal damage cost of unabated pollution waste, from which the consumers or people of the society will suffer at the level $\overline{W}$, would be equal to the marginal cost of abatement of the various wastes as indicated by t. The environmental damage costs due to externalities from unabated wastes have not, however, been explicitly incorporated in the model. The vector t, as observed in an economy, can be conceived as a marginal defensive cost for environmental protection or equivalently as a measure of the valuation of marginal environmental degradation (marginal damage cost) for some assumed preference of the people for environmental quality, which warrants the actual unabated waste flow to be the social optimal. Once the technology, the conventional primary factor prices and the natural capital prices are given, the marginal cost of abatement, which is independent of the scale of abatement for the above model, would determine the environmental standard in terms of $\overline{W}$, where it is equated with the marginal damage cost. While this optimal standard would correspond to the EK_s of the preceding section, the position of the marginal damage value function would, however, be influenced by the past degradation of the environment (ΔEK_3) so that the $\overline{W}$ takes account of part of the requirement of restoration of environmental capacity to EK_s that is, $\Delta EK_3 = EK_s - EK_{T-1}$. The t vector can, in fact, be treated as an environmental pollution tax that the polluter will have to pay for disposing any unabated waste into the sink as a price of the sink service of nature for the control of the damages from flow of wastes at the socially optimal level.

The demand–supply balances of products and factor inputs, and the competitive cost price conditions, however, give us the following identity between the expenditure and factor income methods based estimates of GDP. This is obtained by pre-multiplying both sides of Equations (7), (8), (9) and (10) by the respective vectors p, t, v and π, and post-multiplying both sides of Equations (11) and (12) by X and Z, respectively and setting at equality the alternative expressions of $pX + tZ$. We obtain the final result as:

$$pF + t\left(W^f - \overline{W}\right) = vb + \pi r \tag{13a}$$

$$\text{Or } pF + tW^f = vb + \pi r + t\overline{W}. \tag{13b}$$

The GDP would thus be $pF + tW^f$, the value of final expenditure on goods and services including the share of waste disposal of such final uses. This is equivalent to the total factor incomes arising from the use of primary factors of labour and capital in the forms of wages and profits or return to man-made capital, the natural resources in the form of rent or royalty and that of the sink service of nature in the form of environmental taxes imposed for waste disposal at the rate of marginal abatement costs.

How much would the estimate of GDP vary in our above formulation because of the incorporation of environmental concerns? In the case of abundance of environmental capacity or neglect of environmental concerns, the actual or perceived environmental capacity is considered to be so large that the natural resources are treated as free goods implying $\pi = 0$, and there is no need for restriction on the disposal of unabated polluting waste into the sink, that is, $\overline{W}$ can be of any value with $Z=0$ in Equation (8), that is, $\overline{W} = W_1 X + W^f$.

In actual reality, the natural resources are not always intrinsically treated as free goods, and the users often pay some rent or royalty, though such rent, as charged, is not always consistent with the sustainable patterns of the use of the resources, as would be implied by the maintenance of EK_s over time. It is only in a situation of rational expectation behaviour of the users of resources that the correct supporting sustainable or socially optimal prices π will be expected and actually be realized. This is not often the reality and the political economy of resource use results in the overuse of resources. For similar reasons, though the actual environmental protection measures undertaken by pollution abatement are positive, they fall short of the socially optimal level of abatement.

The comparative use of resources and waste flow under the alternative conditions of abundant capacity, sustainable use of environmental capacity and the actual situation of overuse of environmental capacity are depicted in the following two diagrams, that is, Figures 2 and 3, depicting natural resource use and pollution abatement, respectively.

FIGURE 2

Natural resource use

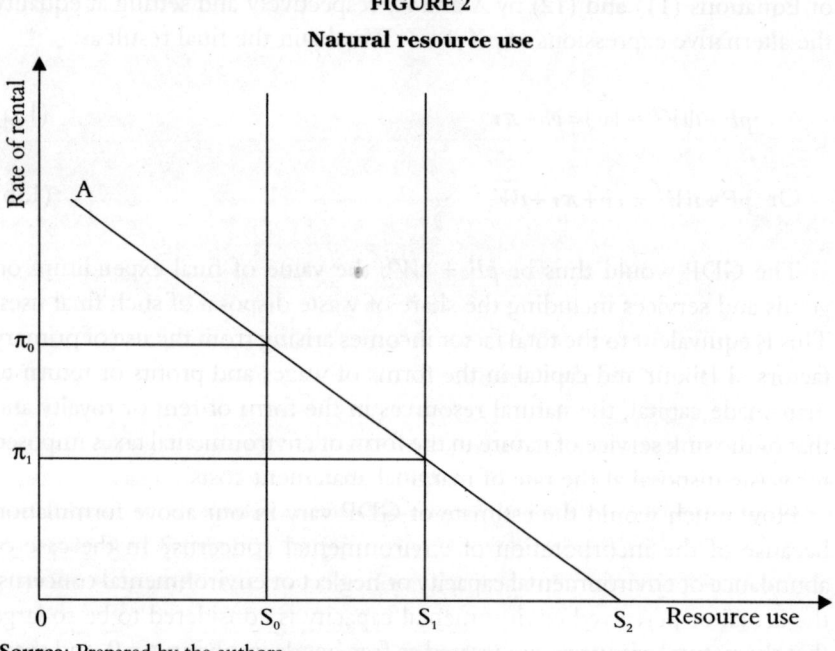

Source: Prepared by the authors.

In Figure 2, AS_2 shows the equilibrium use of a resource in the multi-sectoral macroeconomy for the different resource price or resource rentals. If the sustainable price of the scarce resource be π_0, then OS_0 will be the sustainable use of the resource, which is warranted by the optimal theory of resource use—renewable or non-renewable—over time. However, if the

FIGURE 3
Pollution flows and abatement

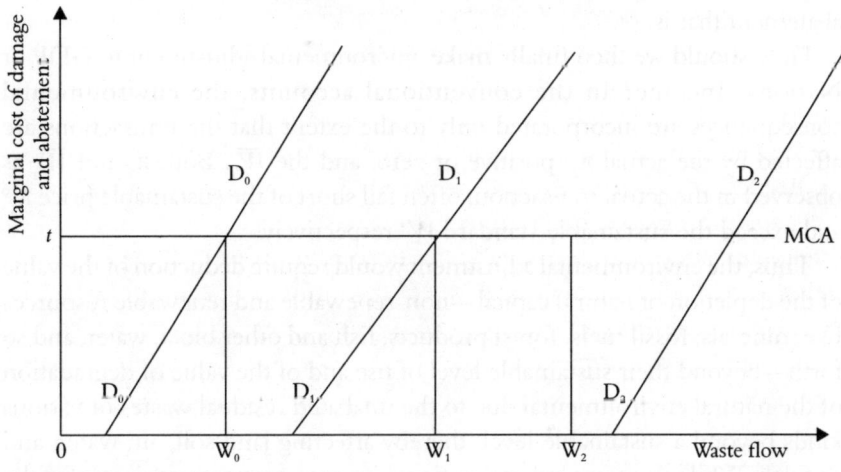

Source: Prepared by the authors.

perceived resource scarcity is less than the true scarcity as determined by the natural growth of a renewable resource or the cost price of use of the alternative resource and the associated backstop technology for an exhaustible resource, the resource rental may prevail at π_1, causing the use of OS_1, which is in excess of OS_0 by the amount of S_0S_1. In a situation of resource abundance, the resource price should be zero and its use will go up to OS_2. The sustainable resource accounting will attempt to adjust the income and the total value added for the depletion of the resource, which is equivalent to S_0S_1 in Figure 2 at the appropriate prices.

Similarly, in Figure 3, the waste flow in the macroeconomy, in the absence of any control of emission, is given to be OW_2 and the marginal cost of abatement as $0t$. The curves D_0D_0, D_1D_1 and D_2D_2 describe the marginal cost of environmental damage curves due to externalities for the respective situations of sustainable environmental capacity, the perceived environmental capacity (which is over-estimated to be in excess of the sustainable level), and that of environmental capacity abundance for waste absorption. While the restoration to the truly sustainable environmental capacity will require an optimal abatement of W_0W_2 with environmental standard $= OW_0$, the actual abatement would be W_1W_2 with unabated emission $= OW_1$ causing under-abatement or environmental degradation beyond the sustainable level by an amount W_0W_1. In a hypothetical situation of environmental capacity abundance, there would, however, be no abatement of pollution and the waste flow will remain as OW_2. The sustainable environmental accounting will require adjustment of the income or net domestic product for the environmental degradation to the extent of W_0W_1 at the marginal cost of abatement, that is, $0t$.

How should we then finally make environmental adjustment to GDP or National Income? In the conventional accounts, the environmental consequences are incorporated only to the extent that the transactions are affected by the actual π_1, positive or zero, and the $\overline{W}_s$. Both π_1 and $\overline{W}_s$ as observed in the actual transaction, often fall short of the sustainable price π_1^0 and exceed the sustainable standard W_s^* respectively.

Thus, the environmental adjustment would require deduction of the value of the depletion of natural capital—non-renewable and renewable resources like minerals, fossil fuels, forest products, fish and other biota, water, and so forth—beyond their sustainable level of use and of the value of degradation of the natural environmental due to the unabated residual wastes of various kinds beyond a sustainable level, thereby affecting land soil, air, water, and so forth. While the conventional national income accounting adjusts for the depreciation of man-made capital, which is included in v_k for k = man-made capital, it does not make any adjustment of income for the natural capital depletion or degradation for sustainability. If K be the physical stock of the primary factor (k) man-made capital and p_k be its price, then $V_k=(\delta+i)p_kK$, where δ is the rate of depreciation and i the rate of interest or normal rate of return on man-made capital employed in the macroeconomy. The NDP is obtained from Gross Value Added or GDP by subtracting δp_kK. In order to obtain environmentally adjusted NDP, we need to work out for each major type of natural capital the counterparts of δ and p_k. In other words, we have to assess the extent of physical depletion or degradation and the accounting prices to be used for assessing the depletion or degradation with reference to the sustainable level of environmental capacity. With reference to Equation (13b), the NDP can then be expressed as follows:

$$NDP=pF + tW^f - \delta p_kK - \pi(r-r^*) - t(Z + \overline{W} - W^*) \qquad (14)$$

where $\delta p_k K$ is the depreciation of man-made capital, $\pi(r-r^*)$, the depletion of natural resource stocks and $t(Z + \overline{W} - W^*)$ is the total provision for degradation of the natural environmental capacity due to waste flow; r^* and W^* being the vectors of sustainable levels of resource use and waste flows, and r and $\overline{W}$ the vectors of actual resource use and unabated waste flow.

The above adjustments necessitate the setting up of an asset account of a macroeconomy including both man-made and natural capital with appropriate classification showing the changes that occurred during the current year due to factors like capital formation, natural growth, their consumption or degradation in production, or other variations, and so forth. It is the reduction in the values due to the production account, which would only need to be adjusted to estimate national income as a sustainable flow of maximum possible consumption in the Hicksian sense. The integration of environment and economic accounting will require the careful linking of the two accounts to provide one integrated picture of the income and wealth of a nation.

9. Classification of Natural Resources

The resource accounting of the natural environment requires classification and inventorization of the different types of natural assets and their valuation. It may be noted that we need to account for the undeveloped or unmanaged resources (uncultivated biological resources, like wild fish or timber of uncultivated forests, unproved but inferred sub-soil assets or reserves, air, water bodies, and so forth) as well as the developed ones. It is, in fact, important to monitor and assess the value of resource transfer from the undeveloped to the developed state for the interlinking of the resources at the different stages of development and use. The valuation of developed natural assets would consist of: (*a*) the scarcity value of such in-place resources with intrinsic values as well as (*b*) the development cost for getting it transferred from the undeveloped to the developed category or from the natural environment to the economic environment. The development cost is generally capitalized and treated as man-made capital of the concerned producing sector using the resource. For example, land development cost would be part of man- made capital in agriculture, or the discovery cost of sub-soil asset would be part of the man-made capital cost of the oil extraction industry. The in-place value of the natural resource (net of any development cost) also undergoes changes due to increasing knowledge about the properties of these resources while they are being developed or due to changes in technology or price conditions. These changes also warrant revaluation of such natural assets from time to time. As the different natural assets have different types of characteristics and range of end-uses, which would influence the valuation rule of their environmental services, it is important to ascertain their classification and then inventorise and evaluate them accordingly.

The major classification of resources that is relevant for the choice of method of measuring physical stocks as well as that of valuation is the broad classification into: (1) stock flow resource, and (2) fund flow resource (Daly and Farley 2003). The stock flow resources are the ones which are depleted and used up in the processes of production as they are materially transformed into what they produce, for example, fossil fuels, mineral resources, forest woods for timber, water for agriculture and other biotic products like fish stocks, cattle for slaughter, and so forth. Such resources, are in fact, the *material cause* of the concerned products. All exhaustible and biotic or abiotic harvestable renewable resources fall in this category. The principle of valuation of these would be given by the rental value of these resources as arising from a pattern of extraction or harvesting of such resources. The rate of depletion of such a resource can be any number per unit of time, high or low, and can be expressed in terms of units of the resource depleted or harvested.

The fund flow resources are, on the other hand, the ones that cannot be physically depleted nor be used up in production, but can provide a flow of service to the production processes and the society. These assets are the *efficient cause* of production. The examples of such resources are air, water bodies, land, forest providing eco-services as watershed, biodiversity, microclimate control, and so forth. Any component of an ecosystem resource, which provides the sink service of waste absorption, is to be treated as a fund flow resource. Such fund flow resource can take place at a given rate per unit of time and be measured accordingly. Its measure would be in terms of some time rate of output service or a qualitative change of such resource, say, receiving so much pollution for degradation in the water body per unit of time.

The stock flow resources of nature have further been classified into biotic resources (fish stock, trees for timber) and abiotic resources (drinking water, fossil fuel, and so forth). While all the biological resources are renewable, the abiotic resources may be both renewable (like water or soil) and non-renewable. The stock flow or fund service flow character and the renewability or non-renewability of resources would matter in our choice of valuation methods.

10. Valuation of Natural Resources

10.1 Exhaustible Resource

The valuation of in-place resource of an exhaustible stock flow resource would follow the rate of rental as per the net price approach of Hotelling (1931). In other words, the excess of price (P) over the marginal cost (MC) of extraction is to be imputed to a unit of the resource at the margin. If Q be the quantity extracted of the resource, then the total depletion value should be $(P - MC)Q$. We assume here that the sustainable level of resource extraction is zero. If a new resource of $\overline{Q}$ is discovered, then the net value of depletion to be considered would be $(P - MC)(Q - \overline{Q})$.

The alternative approach of estimating the depletion value of exhaustible resources as given by El Serafy has been the user's cost approach (El Serafy 1991). As per this approach, the true income from an exhaustible resource is the annuitized income in perpetuity of the resource rents to be arising in the different years of the remaining life of an exhaustible resource stock. If an amount of R of rent, (that is, sales value minus all other factor costs of production) is earned in each of $n+1$ number of the remaining years of the resource deposits, and if X be the true annuitised income in perpetuity, then

$R - X = \dfrac{R}{(1+i)^{n+1}}$ would be the user's cost of depletion in each of the remaining $n+1$ period, 'i' being the rate of interest or discount.[1] It is not difficult to see that if this depreciation provision is invested every year of the remaining life of the resource stock, there would arise an income of X in perpetuity. $R - X$ should then be the provision for depreciation as per the Hicksian concept of sustainable income from the resource.

The Hotelling rule and El Serafy's rule of valuation would, however, yield the same result of depletion value if the rate of rental of the resource is assumed to grow at the rate of interest as per Hotelling's theory of resource rent supporting optimal depletion (Hartwick and Hageman 1993). In any case, the deduction of such value is to be shown in the National Product and Wealth Account to obtain the true changes in the values of exhaustible abiotic resources. The net investment would be represented by the exploration less depletion of the stocks as valued at the rate of per unit Hotelling rent or the user's cost to obtain an estimate of sustainable income in the national accounts. This may be a positive or negative value.

---

[1] Let the extraction of a mineral reserve with the remaining life of $n+1$ period yield a uniform rent R over this time horizon. Let V be the present value of the mine and X be the annuity income equivalent in perpetuity of the rent earned over the life of the $n+1$ period. Let i be the rate of interest or discount. Thus,

$$V = R + \frac{R}{(1+i)} + \frac{R}{(1+i)^2} + \ldots\ldots + \frac{R}{(1+i)^{n+1}}$$

$$= \frac{R(1+i)}{i}\left\{1 - \frac{1}{(1+i)^{n+1}}\right\} \tag{1}$$

Again $V = \dfrac{(1+i)}{i} X$ (2)

From (1) and (2), $R - X = \dfrac{R}{(1+i)^{n+1}}$

10.2 Renewable Resource

In the case of biotic renewables, the broad principle of evaluation has followed the same rule of net price, that is, excess of price (P) over marginal cost (MC) of the resource as applied to the net growth, that is, biotic growth (G) less the quantum of harvest or resource use R. The total valuation of the net growth of such renewable stock would be $(P - MC)(G - R)$ or that of net depletion would be $(P - MC)(R - G)$ which will correspond equivalently to $\pi(r - r^*)$ of Equation 13 in Section 8. However, the question arises as to what should be valued as depletion from the sustainability viewpoint as the pre-existing stock may exceed or fall short of the steady state level of stock of the renewable biotic resource. While in steady state, there will be no change in stock, there will be positive or negative physical net growth of such resource stock when the system is not in a steady state. These changes in values need to be appropriately incorporated in the product and wealth accounts of the national accounts system as in the case of exhaustible resources.

For abiotic renewable resources like groundwater which is a stock flow resource and may be depleted due to over-extraction, the rental value of the resource and its changes can be derived from the marginal value contribution of water in the concerned end-use. Soil is again an abiotic renewable resource, the nutrient being its material content. The fund flow resource of land can also wear out if mismanagement causes its air or water erosion or its nutrient depletion because of over-use. All these may affect the Ricardian rent of the concerned land given by the net price method, whose capitalized value gives its price. One has to estimate the partial effect of soil erosion on the resource rent of land from the cross-section variation of land prices by an appropriate econometric analysis. The valuation of all these resources which are private goods, or natural attributes of some private good (like the nutrient of soil of a land) follow the net price method using market prices and costs of production of the resource using sector.

10.3 Sink Service Resource

As far as the valuation of the sink service of nature—land, air or water—is concerned, we essentially have to estimate the value of the damage of externality due to deterioration of its quality caused by pollution externalities. Such damage results in the depletion of the regenerative capacity of the concerned ecosystem of the fund flow resource. The offsite effects of the externalities of soil degradation due to erosion or pollution also come under this category of sink service degradation. In view of the non-market character of the sink service of the nature, it is difficult and challenging to estimate such damage. In the accounting context, we would consider the quantitative impact of economic activities in terms of residual pollutant arisings and estimate the monetized values of their impact of damage for adjustments in the macro-aggregates of true income and wealth. Environmental economics literature provides broadly two alternative methodological approaches for such valuation: (a) Maintenance cost approach and (b) Willingness to pay approach.

The maintenance or defensive cost approach estimates the total and marginal cost of pollution abatement (reduction of pollutant flow to the sink) for the restoration or upgradation of the quality of air shed or water body, landfill, and so forth to offset the damage. Such estimates of value would include the depreciation value of degradation of the assets.

The alternative approach of willingness to pay for improved quality of air or water or land gives an estimate of the marginal and total benefit that the sufferers of externalities would derive from such improvement. The literature provides two alternative methods—one of revealed preference and the other of stated preference—to estimate the total or marginal willingness to pay for the change in the environmental quality of the sink. The revealed preference method estimates the offer price by an individual for varying environmental quality (with the other factors remaining unchanged), by analyzing the relation between the variation of asset prices and other transaction expenditure on travel, income, health care, and so forth, and that of the associated environmental quality and other relevant socio-economic factors from some observed sample data. The Hedonic pricing, travel cost and health production-function methods are such illustrative methods.

The contingent valuation method of environmental quality, on the other hand, has evolved, to find out the same willingness to pay by generating and analyzing data through a primary survey of households or the concerned units who are the sufferers of externalities, by directly asking them to state their preferences in terms of the payment offer for improvement, or compensation demand for the damage of the environment. The valuation of improvement of environmental quality (a public good) is to be obtained from the survey data on individual offer prices for such changes, individual income and other socio-economic factors and related variables through appropriate econometric analysis and aggregation.

As per the socially optimal allocation of resources for such public good supply of environmental quality variation, the marginal willingness to pay would be equal to the marginal defensive cost or cost of abatement for restoration of the environmental capacity to the socially optimum level, irrespective of the precise method chosen to estimate the former. This has been the rationale behind the use of the defensive or maintenance cost approach in the environmental adjustment of macroeconomic indicators of NDP as discussed in the later sections, particularly in view of the wide variation in the estimates that are often obtained by the alternative methods of estimation of willingness to pay due to the different degrees of influence of subjective elements in the associated survey data generating process.

It should, however, be noted here that mitigation of the damage effect of the residual waste can be facilitated in two alternative ways:

(a)   By incurring avoidance cost through the structural adjustment of technology, resource substitution, and changing of product-mix and GDP;

(b)   By incurring abatement of pollution and restoration cost without changing or stopping any production activity.

In the former case, the total output and GDP may go down, while in the latter case, the same may go up as the economy has to embark on new activities of treating or inhibiting the pollution. It is the defensive cost for abating pollution for a given level of the final output of sectors other than that of the environmental protection industry, which is considered appropriate for describing the provision for the depreciation of environmental capacity of the economy as per the Hicksian concept of sustainable income. We may consider the value of degradation for a given situation of an economy for a year to be the maintenance cost, that is, $\psi\left(W-\overline{W}\right)+\left\{t\times\left(\overline{W}-W^*\right)\right\}$, where W, $\overline{W}$ and W^* are the actual gross waste, net waste (after abatement), and waste or emission flow as per sustainability standard, respectively, and $\psi(W-\overline{W})$ is the actual total abatement cost (ψ being functional notation), and 't' the marginal cost of abatement.

11. Physical Flow Account

The sustainable accounting of the income and wealth of a nation thus requires classified inventorization of various natural assets to monitor their opening stocks, the changes during a period and the closing stocks in both quantity and value terms, and also the flows of residuals (wastes) from the economy into the environment causing degradation of the latter with value implications of assets. One of the important building blocks for sustainable resource accounting has been the development of physical flow accounts showing the flows of all kinds of physical substances constituting natural resources, ecosystem inputs, products and residual wastes. These material substances flow from the origins of (i) the natural environment of the national economy, (ii) the rest of the world (ROW) natural environment, (iii) the different industrial and final use sectors of the national economy, and those of (iv) the ROW economy to the destinations of:

- the sectors of the national economy
- the ROW economy
- the natural environment of the national economy and that of
- the ROW.

Following the UNSD's SEEA 2003 Manual, we present below the physical flow account in a summary format to provide a comprehensive overview of all kinds of physical flows in common use. It would, however, be highly ambitious to attempt to implement such comprehensive accounts, nor would it be necessary for particular aspects of the study of macroeconomics and the environment for which these are mostly developed for use. Different countries have, in fact, implemented such accounts to different extent of coverage and details.

It may be noted, first of all that the SEEA has classified the physical flows of four types of physical substances:

(a) *Natural resource inputs*: These are drawn into the economy and transformed into products, covering minerals, energy resources, water, soil and biological resources. These resource inputs are marketable.

(b) *Ecosystem inputs*: These are substances which are directly absorbed from the ecosystem for the purposes of production and consumption in the economy, such as water and other natural inputs like nutrients, oxygen, carbon dioxide, etc., that are required by plants and animals for growth, or oxygen for combustion, etc., with direct or implicit prices payable depending on the property rights structure on the sources of such resources like watershed or land, etc. However, there should not be double counting in natural resource and ecosystem input accounting. For example, if irrigation water is abstracted from water body and shown as a natural resource, it should not be counted as an ecosystem input. It may also be noted that the ecosystem inputs are distinct from ecosystem services, which are much wider and include, for example, the assimilative capacity of the environment and the provision of biodiversity.

(c) *Products*: These cover goods and services produced within the economic sphere and used within it, including those flowing between the national economy and the ROW economy, that is, exports and imports.

(d) *Residuals*: These are the undesired by-product outputs of the economy that have zero value to the generator. These may be recycled or reused or treated for the abatement of the harmful pollutant contents, and can have positive value to other economic agents as they flow.

A schematic matrix presentation of the physical flows of an economy in notational terms is given in Table 2. A numerical illustrative presentation of the flows for a hypothetical economy is shown in Table 3 in summary form. The detailed data on the component sub-matrices of this table of physical flows are available in UNSD's handbook '*Integrated Environmental and Economic Accounting: An Operational Manual*', 2003 (www.unstats.un.org/unsd/envaccounting/seea.htm), which one may refer to. All figures in Tables 2 and 3 are expressed in million tonne units, the material balance column showing the excess of the concerned column totals over the row totals, which would represent net accumulation in the economy or in the natural environment. The SEEA source from which the flow matrix has been taken and aggregated, classifies the production activities into three sectors—primary, secondary (industry) and tertiary services. These sectoral activities include the natural resource extraction activities as well as the environmental management and protection activities, which may however be shown separately. The choice of the level of aggregation would depend on the context and purpose of the macroeconomic level study for which the table is being set up. The products have been classified into aggregate groups in the SEEA matrices of physical flows depending on the material and pollution intensities.

The SEEA matrix of physical flow for a hypothetical economy has treated all consumption by household and government as one, and all capital formation as another final use activity sector for presentation. Finally, the ROW is a sector making the final use of products and use of natural resources and receiving residuals, which are supplied as exports from the economy. This sector, on the other hand, supplies products, natural resources and wastes, which are imports to the economy.

12. Hybrid Flow Accounts

In order to analyze the environmental implications of the macroeconomic value aggregates which are used to monitor the performance of an economy, it is now important to juxtapose these physical flow accounts data with the corresponding monetary flow accounts data presented in the same format. In view of the non-availability of market price data for many of the resource and residual flows from and to the natural environment, some countries

TABLE 2

Schematic matrix presentation of the physical flows between the economy and the environment

Origin ↓ / Destination →	Economy — Products	Economy — Industries	Economy — Consumption	Economy — Capital formation	Natural environment / residuals — Exports to ROW	Natural environment / residuals — National destination	Natural environment / residuals — ROW	Material balance	Total
Economy — Products		A	f^c	f^I	x				*
Industries	Y					W	x_w	b_i	*
Consumption						w^c	x_w^c	b_l	*
Capital formation						w^f	x_w^I	b_m	*
ROW origin imports	m					w_m			*
Natural Environment — Natural resources — National origin		R	f_r^c		x_r			t_r	*
Natural resources — ROW origin		m_r	m_r^c	–	–			b_{mr}	*
Ecosystem inputs — National origin		r_e	r_e^c		x_e			t_e	*
Ecosystem inputs — ROW origin		m_e^c	m_e^c	–				b_{mc}	*
Residuals — National origin		Z	–	Z^I		m_w^b	x_w^b	t_w	*
Residuals — ROW origin								b_{mw}	*
Total	*	*	*	*	*	*	*	∞	*

Source: Prepared by the authors.

TABLE 3

An illustrative matrix representation of physical flows (summary table)

(million tonnes)

	Economy					Residual		Material balance	Total use
	1. Products	2. Industries	3. Consumption	4. Capital	5. ROW (destination)	10. National destination	11. ROW destination		
1. Products		Products used by industry 442.000	Products used for consumption 39.000	Products used for capital 119.000	Products used by ROW (Exports) 101.000				701.000
2. Industries	Products supplied by industry 551.000					Residuals generated by industry 275.258	Residuals generated by industry in ROW 4.587		830.845
3. Consumption						Residuals generated by consumption 47.461	Residuals generated by consumption in ROW 0.745	Net material accumulation by consumption 16.794	65.000
4. Capital						Residuals generated by capital 72.595		Net material accumulation by capital 72.215	144.810
5. ROW (origin)	Products supplied by ROW (imports) 150.000					Residuals generated by non-residents 5.756		Net material accumulation by ROW economy –51.756	104.000

Economy

(Table 3 continued)

	Economy					Residual		Material balance	Total use
	1. Products	2. Industries	3. Consumption	4. Capital	5. ROW (destination)	10. National destination	11. ROW destination		
Natural resources									
6. National environment		Natural resources supplied to industry 256.000	Natural resources supplied to consumption 1.000		Natural resources extracted by ROW 1.000			Net accumulation of natural resources in the national environment −258.000	Net
7. ROW origin		Natural resources supplied to industry 5.000	Natural resources supplied to consumption 1.000					Net accumulation of natural resources in the ROW −6.000	0
Ecosystem inputs									
8. National environment		Ecosystem inputs to industry 118.00	Ecosystem inputs to consumption 23.000		Ecosystem inputs to ROW economy	2.000		Net accumulation of ecosystem inputs in the national environment −143.000	0
9. ROW origin		Ecosystem inputs to industry 3.000	Ecosystem inputs to consumption 1.000					Net accumulation of ecosystem inputs in the ROW −4.000	0

(Table 3 continued)

(Table 3 continued)

(million tonnes)

	Economy					Residual		Material balance	Total use
	1. Products	2. Industries	3. Consumption	4. Capital	5. ROW (destination)	10. National destination	11. ROW destination		
Residuals 10. National origin		Residuals reabsorbed by production 6.854		Waste to landfill sites 25.810			Cross boundary residual out-flows 3.919	Net accumulation of residuals in the national environment 372.717	409.291
11. ROW origin					Cross boundary residual in-flows 8.221			Net accumulation of residuals by ROW 1.030	
Total supply	701.000	830.845	65.000	144.810	409.291		9.251	0.000	2264.197

Source: UNSD (2003).

like the Netherlands, developed hybrid account following the basic principles developed by Leontief (1970) and others (Ayres and Kneese 1969; Cumberland 1966; Daly 1968; Isard et al. 1967; Victor 1972). These accounts present the national accounts data and the physical flow accounts data relating to natural resource/ecosystem input use and generation/absorption of residuals in a single matrix. It presents the physical flows in a manner that facilitates comparison of the environmental burden with economic benefits or environmental benefits with economic costs. Such accounts are also useful pointers to the influence of the economic structure on the specific environmental indicators, the policy implications for environmental conservation and trade-offs between environmental and economic strategies for such environmental controls. Such hybrid accounts are useful for working out the environmental consequences of alternative patterns of growth and development, environmental themes like the greenhouse effect, the depletion of the ozone layer, acidification, eutrophication, accumulation of waste and wastewater, and development of suitable models based on the data of such hybrid accounts over time. Such account also points to the need for the development of an environmental and scientific statistical database to facilitate the analysis of proper environment-economy interaction.

In order to convert a physical flow account into a hybrid one, we need to express the flows of the matrices of supply and use of products into value ones at some constant basic prices net of tax, and show the balancing row of value added, which constitutes payments for labour and return to man-made capital employed in the different production sectors. An additional row of product taxes is also shown to obtain the macro-aggregate of GDP at market prices from the GDP at constant factor prices. The matrices of natural resource/ecosystem flows and residuals would, however, remain unchanged and be expressed in physical units only.

Table 4 shows the schematic framework of the hybrid account of the supply and use of products, resources and residuals in terms of notational matrices, while Table 5 gives the monetary flows of supply and use. The illustrative values of the matrices of the hypothetical SEEA economy are given in Table 5.

Countries like the Netherlands, Canada and Germany have focused on the development of a hybrid economic and environmental accounting matrix (NAMEA, CSERA and GEEA, respectively)[2] and have developed several indicators of energy and resource efficiency, and those of environmental

---

[2] NAMEA: National Accounting Matrix including Environmental Accounts (see CBS Statistics Netherlands 2006); CSERA: Canadian System of Environmental and Resource Accounts (see Statistics Canada 2000); GEEA: German System of Environmental–Economic Accounting (see Federal Statistical Office Germany 2006).

TABLE 4

Schematic presentation of the hybrid account of physical-cum-monetary flows of supply and use

Origin↓ Destination→	Economy					Natural environment/ residuals		Material balance	Total
	Products	Industries	Consumption	Capital formation	Exports to ROW	National destination	ROW		
Economy									
Products		A	f^c	f^I	x				*
Trade margin	t_m								
Product taxes	t_x			t_I					
Industries	Y					W	x_w		*
Consumption						w^{fc}	x_w^c	b_c	*
Capital formation						w^f_I	x_w^I	b_I	*
ROW origin imports	m					w_m		b_m	*
Value added		v							*
Natural environment									
Natural resources — National origin		R	r^c_y		x_r			b_r	*
Natural resources — ROW origin		m_r	m^c_r		—			b_{mr}	*
Ecosystem inputs — National origin		r_e	r^c_e		x_e			b_e	*
Ecosystem inputs — ROW origin		m_e	m^c_e		—			b_{me}	*
Residuals — National origin		Z		Z^I		m^b_w	x^b_w	b_w	*
Residuals — ROW origin								b_{mw}	*
Total	*	*	*	*	*	*	*		*

Source: Prepared by the authors.

Note: The italicized notational figures for the matrices and vectors A, Y, m, f^c, f^r, f^I, x and for the additional vectors, that is, value added v, trade margin t_m, indirect taxes net of subsidies for products t_x and t_I for taxes on investment indicate all monetary values. The other entries of the hybrid flow table are in physical terms.

TABLE 5

An illustrative monetary flow of supply and use table

(Billion currency units)

	Economy															
	Products								Industries				Consumption	Capital	Exports	Total
	P1	P2	P3	P4	P5	P6	P7	P	I1	I2	I3	I	C	CF	X	Total
Products																
P1 Animal and vegetable products									0.7	68.0	3.2	72.0	12.8	0.0	20.8	105.6
P2 Stone gravel and building materials									3.5	50.0	1.0	54.5	1.0		4.5	60.0
P3 Energy									47.0	133.4	30.0	210.4	24.1	0.0	137.8	372.3
P4 Metals, machinery. etc.										32.0		32.0	1.5	66.5	45.0	145.0
P5 Plastic and plastic products										4.2		4.2	0.6		0.8	5.6
P6 Wood, paper, etc.										10.1	6.0	16.1	2.0	0.0	6.0	24.0
P7 Other product groups									26.6	213.4	34.8	274.8	464.4	79.5	188.2	1006.9
All Products									**77.8**	**511.2**	**75.0**	**664.0**	**506.4**	**146.0**	**403.0**	**1719.4**
Industries																
Trade margins	9.4	7.8	17.5	6.0	0.6	2.1	-43.5									
Product taxes	0.6	2.4	13.9	1.9	0.3	0.9	50.0	70.0							1.0	
I1 Agriculture, fishing and mining	39.4	18.0	132.9			2.2	36.9	229.4								
I2 Manufacturing, electricity and construction	45.0	26.6	125.1	67.2	2.0	16.8	407.4	690.0								
I3 Services							367.0	367.0								
I Total industries	**84.4**	**44.6**	**258.0**	**67.2**	**2.0**	**19.0**	**811.3**	**1286.4**								
ROW																
Imports of products	11.2	5.2	82.9	70.0	2.8	1.9	189.0	363.0								
Value added									151.6	178.8	292.0	622.4				
Total	105.6	60.0	372.3	145	5.6	24.0	1006.9	1719.4	229.4	690.0	367.0	1286.4				

Source: UNSD (2003).

Note: This table gives the monetary supply and use tables of the economy comprising only the concerned sub-matrices of Table 2.

stress for the purpose of policy analysis based on quantitative and econometric models using the data of such accounts. Such analyses based on the expenditure flows of national accounts as juxtaposed against the gross and net physical flows of residuals in the hybrid account, in fact, provide important results regarding compliance with the environmental standard, the extent of adequacy of actual protection and also of the standards used, and the policy needs. Environmental policy theme-wise macro-modelling based on hybrid accounts has been considered by these countries to be more important and reliable for the development of insights into the sustainable development policies than immediate attempts to adjust macroeconomic aggregates like GDP or NDP. The latter adjustments require comprehensive and reliable valuation estimates of various non-marketable environmental resources and services, which may not presently be available in many countries.

13. Asset Accounts

The basic model of SEEA, however, focuses on how natural resources and ecosystem inputs flow into the economy and how the products and residuals are generated in the production. As the sustainability condition ideally requires the total investment in all kinds of capital assets to be non-negative, sustainable accounting requires the development of an asset account of the economy comprising the man-made capital assets, fixed capital and inventory capital, and the natural capital assets, which are essential for the sustainability of economic processes. However, SNA 1993 delimited the scope of coverage of assets including environmental ones, to the economic assets, which were required to satisfy the following two conditions:

(a) Property rights should be defined on the asset at the level of the individual, state, institution or community.

(b) Its value should be defined in terms of a flow of income or monetary benefit that it would generate over time.

These environmental assets are classified first of all into produced assets and non-produced assets. The produced environmental assets would consist of all cultivated biological assets like livestock, fish, fowl, orchards, plantations, standing agricultural crops, and so forth. Although these are products of photosynthesis and solar energy flows through the food chain and cycles, enormous human energy and capital subsidy have been used in their regeneration and supply. These are, therefore, outputs of production activities of agriculture, fishery, forestry, and so forth. These assets produced would be further classified into fixed assets and inventories. Fixed assets would be such cultivated assets, which are intended for repeated or continuous use in production, for example vineyards, orchards and plantations, livestock for breeding, dairy, draught, and so forth. On the other hand, agricultural standing crops for single use, livestock or fish for slaughter or catch, standing timber waiting to be felled, and so forth, constitute the natural inventory capital of cultivated products. The inventory of produced natural assets would also include the work-in-progress of fixed capital development like uncompleted biological assets under cultivation which would be meant for repeated use once they attain full maturity, live growing plantation or specialized breeder animals, etc. It may be noted here that agricultural crops produced, harvested and sold during a particular period would constitute a product flow, but not an economic asset.

Among the abiotic produced assets, land development should figure as a fixed capital formation. The produced fixed environmental assets also include some intangible asset like mineral exploration. This exploration with the capitalized value of all discovery expenses is an intangible knowledge produced which has been a crucial causal factor for the resource function of this material asset.

Finally, all the produced natural assets are conventional products of economic activities having market values and they already figure in the conventional national accounting system. However, a majority of environmental assets are non-produced assets wherein valuation is not immediately given by the market but can be derived from the analysis of the environmental and economic data. These assets include land for various uses, fossil fuel reserves, metallic and non-metallic mineral reserves, other sub-soil assets, non-cultivated biological resources (for example, wild fish in a river body or coastal water as growing in a natural ecosystem without any human energy and capital subsidy) and water resources. Soil is an important resource, which was considered to be included in the land it covers, as per SNA 1993. However, it deserves to be treated as an asset by itself, which is associated with land just as the surface water associated with it is treated. As the top-soil is removable and subject to erosion, and soil erosion is a serious threat for sustainable agriculture, its explicit recognition in asset accounting like that of water resource, has been recognized in the latest SEEA asset classification. The Ricardian rent of land is, in fact, attributable to its soil content, its quality and moisture. However, as already noted, land development cost, as capitalized, is to be considered as a man-made or a produced fixed capital asset, and is distinct from the value of land as an environmental asset.

Unlike SNA 1993, the latest update of SEEA classifies ecosystems—terrestrial, aquatic and atmospheric ecosystems—as environmental assets. Although they are not economic assets as per the SNA definition because their measurement and valuation are difficult and the ownership right is not well-defined, it has been considered important to monitor the degradation of the quality of these ecosystems, particularly air, water and land, due to the externalities of residual waste arising from the material flows between the economy and the environment. Such quality of ecosystem assets has been proposed to be quantified in terms of the residual flows as received by the ecosystems, like air shed, water bodies and landfill, and the value of their impact is to be imputed to the degradation of the concerned ecosystems. The accounting for such items has been limited to the changes in terms of the quantities of residual flows only during a period without showing the opening and the closing stocks.

Finally, there are the intangible environmental economic assets, which are related to the benefits of nature's functioning ecosystems. These are the transferable licences and concessions for the exploration of natural resources, permits for the emissions of residuals in the atmosphere, and so forth.

Table 6 presents the asset classification with its SEEA updates as discussed above. While a common item like forest or aquatic resources may appear

TABLE 6
Natural assets classification

1	**Produced assets**
1.1	*Fixed assets*
1.1.1	Tangible man-made fixed assets
1.1.2	Cultivated biological assets like livestock, plantation, etc. for repeated use
1.2	*Intangible fixed assets*—mineral exploration
1.3.1	Inventories—timber, crop and plant resources aquatic resources for harvest, livestock for slaughter
1.3.2	Work in progress of cultivated biological fixed assets
2	**Non-produced assets**
2.1	*Tangible non-produced assets*
2.1.1	Land and surface water body for different uses
2.1.2	Natural resources
2.1.2.1	Sub-soil assets—: Fossil fuels, metallic and non-metallic mineral reserves, etc.
2.1.2.2	Soil
2.1.2.3	Water
2.1.2.4	Non-cultivated biological resources—wild aquatic resources, live fishes and other animals, natural forest resources.
2.1.3	Ecosystems
2.1.4	Intangible non-produced assets like lease for exploration right, tradable permits for emissions, etc.

Source: Prepared by the authors.

under more than one classification category depending on where it arises— cultivated or uncultivated source—or on the basis of its use, such identity of classification would matter in respect of valuation and the sustainability benchmark for use.

Tables 7a and 7b provide illustrative asset accounts of produced and non-produced assets following the updated SEEA principle. Table 7(a) shows for a period, the opening and closing stocks and the changes in the produced assets due to investment or fixed capital formation (which will be acquisition less disposal in cultivated biological assets), inventory changes including the changes in work-in-progress, depreciation and losses due to natural disasters, political and other exogenous reasons not related to economic activities. For the non-produced assets, Table 7(b) shows illustrative figures of changes which would consist of the net effects of depletion due to economic use like mineral extraction, fish catches, water abstraction, etc., other accumulation and other volume changes in a given period. The category of 'other accumulation' would include discoveries of the resource, natural growth net of mortality, replenishment of resources like water due to natural cycle and re-classification of assets due to changes in functions or quality. The re-classification would include transfer of resources like land and other resources from the natural environment to economic use or land reclamation, etc. Some of these variations would be measured by acquisition less disposal if it involves economic transactions as in the case of land, water body, etc. These would also include re-assessment and revaluation of mineral reserves because

TABLE 7(a)

Monetary asset accounts for produced assets (including cultivated natural assets)

| | Agriculture | | Forestry | | | |
	Cultivated assets	Other	Cultivated forest	Other	Other industries	Total
Opening stock	3521	5139	1062	2352	701391	713465
Capital formation:						
Gross fixed capital formation*	274	633		215	86784	87906
Changes in inventories	47	41	128	32	−213	35
Consumption of fixed capital*	−48	−73		−39	−23765	−23925
Other volume changes	−21	−33	−11	−29	−174	−268
Revaluation	−83	106	−52	65	1266	1302
Closing stock	3690	5813	1127	2596	765289	778515

(monetary unit)

Source: UNSD (2000).
Note: *Including land improvement.

TABLE 7(b)

Monetary asset accounts for non-produced economic assets

(monetary units)

	Agricultural land	Forest land	Other land (including built-up and recreational land)	Soil (economic use)	Sub-soil assets fossil fuels	Forest (economic use)	Fishery resources	Groundwater	Other freshwater
Opening stocks	440275	374784	2315578		262315	25261	20017	287	85
Gross fixed capital formation	53	49	393						
Sustainable use						-1990	-2833	-97	-26
Depletion (including soil erosion)	-3	-2	-19	432	-8004	-1807	-421	-21	
Other accumulation	12354	-18804	6449						
Acquisition less disposal of non-produced non-financial assets									
Other	5362	-5001	107527		3802	1996	2905	102	33
Other volume changes	-1787	-625			-922	-393	-131	-8	-2
Revaluation	773	31715	38083		-16130	3727	2187	265	60
Closing stocks	457027	382116	2468010		243486	26791	21724	529	150

Source: UNSD (2000).

of change in technology, prices and new information about their qualitative character, which may make some resource an economic asset that had not been so earlier. The other volume changes, on the other hand would mainly consist of changes due to natural calamity, political upheaval and transfer of resource from the economic environment to the natural environment, not connected with degradation attributed to economic activities.

The development of the asset account is important both in physical and monetary value terms. This is because the physical quantities would indicate the strength of the economy in terms of resource security, while the valuation is also important for integrating economic accounting with the environmental accounting and for estimating the change of the macro aggregate of the value of wealth of a nation. Physical asset account development requires the development of comprehensive resource and environmental statistics and a database, as well as the application of multi-disciplinary scientific knowledge to organize the statistics and make them useful for sustainable accounting. The monetary valuation of the assets, on the other hand, as already discussed in a preceding section, would depend on the marketability of the resource, public good character of the asset, its renewability or non-renewability and various scientific-technological specificity, which would be important in determining the precise formula of rent or royalty of the concerned resource depending on its end-use.

14. Degradation of Assets

The development of asset account, as outlined above, is confined only to the quantitative changes, but not the qualitative degradation which may occur as an environmental consequence of economic activities. It is difficult to measure and monitor the qualitative changes of all the assets regularly, though the residual waste arising or the concentration of pollution like CO_2, NO_x, SO_x, BOD, TSP, P, N, and so forth, may be measurable or estimable. It is, therefore, the inventory of emissions and their damage valuation of flow that are proposed to be estimated as per the scheme of SEEA for the assessment of degradation of the natural assets, particularly the ecosystem assets of air, water and land, as already noted in Section 13. The principle of valuation of degradation has already been discussed in Section 10. Broadly, the SEEA recommends the maintenance cost approach for evaluating the residual flows. As already noted, the maintenance cost comprises the cost of abatement of damage and restoration of environmental capacity as per the marginal cost approach. There is one important difference between the accounting for depletion and degradation. The depletion of an asset is caused by the asset-using sectors and its cost can be allocated among users in proportion to the usage. The degradation of assets is caused due to externalities by sectors that are generating the residuals and may not directly be the users of the degradation asset, for example, the energy industry causing NO_x emissions resulting in the acidification and degradation of forest and aquatic ecosystems though the energy sector is not directly using these degraded assets. This has warranted the treatment and quantification of degradation in terms of the residuals and not the ultimate affected asset. The total damage cost is allocated across sectors in proportion to the emissions, which are determined by their respective material usage and technology.

15. Environmental Adjustment to Flow Accounts

The hybrid flow account of any economy gave us the environmental resource and residual flows in physical amount. These flows provide the basic data for the physical depletion and degradation of the environmental resource base of the economy. The monetary conversion of the physical flows of the environmental materials and degradation due to residual flows would finally permit us to adjust the macro aggregates of income, expenditure and assets. It is true that it may not be possible to ensure adequate coverage of assets for accounting in physical and/or value terms because of the lack of a physical database and difficulty in the reliable monetary valuation of assets because of the non-marketability of many of the environmental resources, particularly the fund flow ones. However, for the feasible extent of extension of the asset boundary, we can derive the aggregate value of both the natural resource and ecosystem resource throughput to yield the estimate of consumption of natural capital—both produced and non-produced— with their allocation among producing sectors, final users and the ROW. The estimates of degradation value, on the other hand, can be assumed on the basis of the maintenance cost of the surrounding ecosystem's environmental quality. The latter could be limited to the extent of provision for the reversal of the damage effect of the residual arising in excess of the sustainability standard. These maintenance costs would be allocated as per the distribution of actual residual maintenance or abatement cost incurred across sectors and various final uses.

We are now in a position to show how the national income and wealth accounts can be environmentally adjusted.

Let $\overline{X}$ = total gross value of output other than environmental control industry, that is pX of Section 8.

IC_o = intermediate cost of production other than that of pollution abatement, = pA_1x of Section 8.

$\overline{Z}$ = total cost of degradation based on maintenance/defensive cost.

IC_z = intermediate cost for pollution abatement sector = pA_2Z of section 8.

CFC_o = fixed capital consumption of industries other than environmental protection.

CFC_z = fixed capital consumption in environmental protection industry.

D_p = total value of depletion of natural resources and ecosystem inputs = $\pi(r-r^*)$ of section 8.

D_g = total value of degradation due to waste arising.

$dpNDP$ = depletion adjusted NDP.

$eaNDP$ = environmentally adjusted NDP.

If we assume that the current expenditures by the industry meet the environmental standard of the economy, then we end up with the following:

$$GDP_o = \overline{X} - IC_o$$
$$GDP_z = \overline{Z} - ICz$$
$$GDP = \overline{X} + \overline{Z} - IC_o - IC_z$$
$$NDP_o = GDP_o - CFC_o = \overline{X} - IC_o - CFC_o$$
$$NDP_z = GDP_z - CFC_z = \overline{Z} - IC_z - CFC_z$$
$$NDP = \overline{X} + \overline{Z} - IC_o - IC_z - CFC_o - CFC_z$$

$$dpNDP = GDP - CFC_o - CFC_z - D_p$$
$$= \overline{X} + \overline{Z} - IC_o - IC_z - CFC_o - CFC_z - D_p$$
$$= eaNDP \text{ (with environmental standard being met)}$$

If, however, the current spending on abatement falls short of the environmental standard, that is, $W > W^*$ then $Dg = \{t \times (\overline{W} - W^*)\} + \psi(W - \overline{W})$ is to be deducted from GDP for the consumption of the environmental capacity of the nature as sink due to inadequate abatement. We should thus have,

$$eaNDP = eaGDP - CFC - D_p - D_g$$

$$= eaNDP - D_g$$
$$= \overline{X} + \overline{Z} - IC_o - IC_z - CFC_o - CFC_z - D_p - D_g$$

If the economy had no spending on environmental maintenance, the gross savings or investment in the economy would have been S_o, where $S_o = GDP - \overline{C}$, where $\overline{C}$ is the total value of consumption. As per the actual expenditure, the estimates of gross savings S and that of genuine net savings Sg would be as follows:

$$S = GDP - \overline{C} = \overline{X} + \overline{Z} - IC_o - IC_z - \overline{C}$$
$$S_g = GDP - CFC - D_p - D_g - \overline{C}$$
$$= \overline{X} + \overline{Z} - IC_o - IC_z - CFC - D_p - D_g - \overline{C}$$

The ratio of S_g to GDP would represent the true saving rate of an economy. It is important to compare the time paths of GDP with eaNDP and that of S or S/GDP with S_g or S_g/GDP, respectively. We may refer to Table 8 showing comparative estimates of genuine savings in various regions of the world as worked out by the World Bank (1999), on the basis of some crude assumptions. The calculation behind the estimates considers educational expenditure as investment spending in human capital while working out the genuine savings. The last column of Table 8 shows the genuine savings gross of educational expenses, which are part of the savings utilized for educational investment, and correspond to the genuine savings as defined above.

As the genuine savings and the genuine investment would be equal in ex-post accounting, it is the sign and magnitude of Sg, which is an indicator of sustainability of the macroeconomy. The ratios Dp/GDP and Dg/GDP would be important indicators of depreciation of the environmental capacity of a country while $(\overline{Z} - ICz)/GDP$ would indicate the environmental control effort of the economy for sustainability.

In order to obtain an overview of the integration of economic and environmental accounting as discussed above, we can bring the production-cum-income account and the asset account together by juxtaposing them against each other. The integrated accounts show the extension of the asset boundary to include various types of natural capital and restructuring of production account, which may show environmental protection activities and products separately within the production account. This depicts the role of economy-environment interaction in determining true income, genuine savings and wealth. While Figure 4 makes a schematic presentation

TABLE 8

Region-wise estimates of genuine savings, 1997

(percentage)

	Gross domestic savings	Consumption of fixed capital	Net domestic savings	Education expenditure	Energy depletion	Mineral depletion	Net forest depletion	Carbon dioxide damage	Genuine domestic savings
World	22.2	11.7	10.5	5.0	1.2	0.1	0.1	0.4	13.6
Low income	17.0	8.0	9.1	3.4	4.2	0.6	1.8	1.2	4.8
Middle income	26.2	9.2	17.0	3.5	3.8	0.5	0.2	1.1	15.0
High income	21.4	12.4	9.0	5.3	0.5	0.0	0.0	0.3	13.5
East Asia and Pacific	38.3	6.9	31.4	2.1	0.9	0.5	0.7	1.7	29.7
Europe and Central Asia	21.4	13.7	7.9	4.2	4.9	0.1	0.0	1.6	5.6
Latin America and Caribbean	20.5	8.3	12.2	3.6	2.7	0.7	0.0	0.3	12.1
Middle East and North Africa	24.1	8.8	15.3	5.2	19.7	0.1	0.0	0.9	−0.3
South Asia	18.2	9.1	9.1	3.8	2.1	0.4	2.0	1.3	7.1
Sub-Saharan Africa	16.8	9.1	7.8	4.5	5.9	1.4	0.5	0.9	3.4

Source: World Bank (1999).

FIGURE 4

SEEA: Flow and stock accounts with environmental assets

			Assets	
			Economic assets	Environmental assets
OPENING STOCKS				
	Industries	Households/ Govt.	+	Rest of the World
SUPPLY OF PRODUCTS	Domestic production			Imports of products
	thereof: for environmental protection			**thereof: for environmental protection**
	Economic cost (intermediate consumption, consumption of fixed capital)	Final consumption	Gross capital formation, consumption of fixed capital	Exports
USE OF PRODUCTS	**thereof: for environmental protection**			**thereof: for environmental protection**
USE OF NATURAL ASSETS	**Environmental cost of industries (imputed)**	**Environmental cost of households (imputed)**	**Natural capital consumption**	

+

	Other changes of economic assets	Other changes of environmental assets
OTHER CHANGES OF ASSETS		

=

	Economic assets	Environmental assets
CLOSING STOCKS		

Source: United Nations Statistics Division (UNSD) (2000).

of the overview of such integrated production-cum-asset account, Table 9 makes a notational presentation of the integrated account in terms of matrix notations.

16. Variants of the SEEA and Implementation of the NRA and SEEA in India

It may be noted that different versions of the SEEA have been developed to facilitate the adaptation of the system in different countries, according to their respective national priorities, environmental concerns and statistical capabilities. The different versions of the SEEA generally adhere to the

TABLE 9
Schematic presentation (Notational) of integrated environmental and economic accounts

	Environmental protection industry	Other industries	Imports	Exports	Consumption	Produced assets	Natural economic assets	Environmental assets
Opening stock						K_o	N_o	
Output	$\bar{Z}$	$\bar{X}$	$-M$	$\bar{EX}$	$\bar{C}$	$\bar{I}$		
Intermediate cost	IC_z	IC_o						
Consumption of fixed capital	CFC_z	CFC_o				$-CFC$		
Resource depletion	Dp_z	Dp_o			Dp_c		Dp	
Degradation maintenance cost	Dg_z	Dg_o			Dg_c			Dg
GDP	GDP_z	GDP_o						
eaNDP	$eaNDP_z$	$eaNDP_o$						
Other accumulation						OA		
Other volume changes						OVC		
Revaluation						RV		
Closing stock						K_T	N_T	

Source: Prepared by the authors.

Note: Dp_z, Dp_o and Dp_c are the sub-matrices of the values of depletion of natural resources due to environmental protection activities, other conventional industries and final consumption in the economy. Dg, Dg_o and Dg_c are the similar respective sectoral estimates of environmental degradation due to residual flows.

production definitions of the SNA, its accounting identities, and its reliance on observed data. It advocates a flexible approach in implementation involving four stages (UNSD 1993). The first version starts with the revised SNA—revising SNA's input-output and asset accounts to present separately environmentally relevant economic activities. The second version involves reformatting and disaggregation of SNA in order to identify environmental protection activities. The third version of development involves adoption of physical resource accounting based on the concepts of material/energy balances and natural resource accounting. The fourth version additionally introduces the estimation of value of natural assets and imputed

FIGURE 5

SEEA versions and links to the 1993 SNA

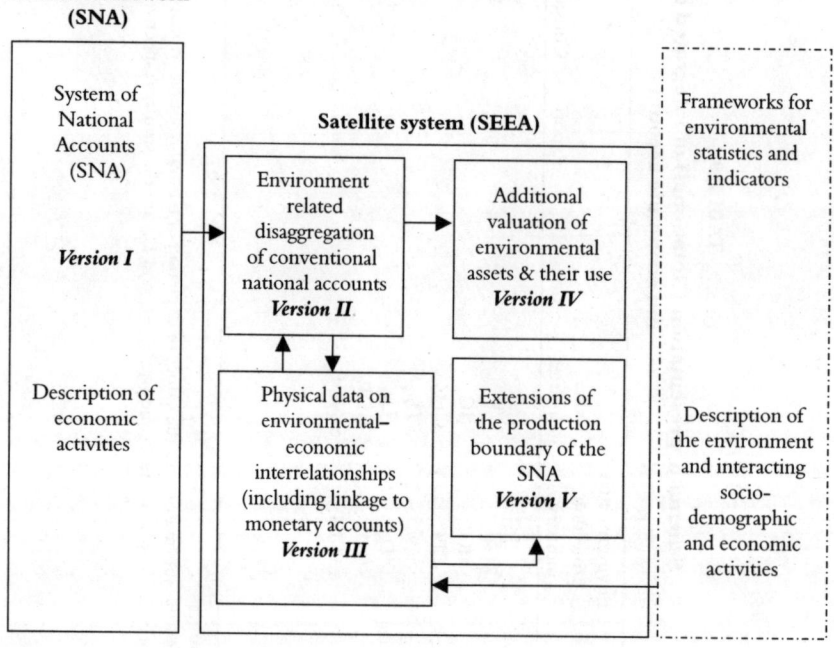

Source: UNSD (2000).

environmental costs through alternative valuation methods. A fifth version, which would allow expansion of the SNA production boundary to include the household activities and the environmental services produced by nature, has not been recommended for adoption by the SEEA proponents (See Figure 5).

Despite the significance of accounting for natural resources in the National Accounts, government-sponsored effort in India to supplement or reform the National Accounts has remained restricted to only the compilation and presentation of environmental statistics in the 'Compendium of Environmental Statistics' since 1997 (see Central Statistical Organization 1997, 2003, 2006). This document contains an inventory of environmental statistics under the six internationally recognized classified categories, that is, flora, fauna, atmosphere, water, land/soil and human settlements, based on the United Nations framework for development of environment. However, the database is compiled from several sources and in many cases, the data are not regularly collected and the statistics remain backdated for several resources. Due to lack of consistent time series data, it is not possible at the current level and state of data collection to construct environmental asset accounts as proposed under the SEEA. Even though the data inventory exists for water and forest resources, no official attempt has been made to construct asset accounts for these resources. However, several academic endeavours of accounting for natural resources in India point to the feasibility of constructing integrated environmental and economic accounts.

The Natural Resource Accounting involves substantive inter-disciplinary research efforts, which would be quite country- and ecosystem-specific. In India, several research initiatives have taken place in the area of environmental impact analysis and valuation of environmental benefits and damages, though these initiatives have not been driven by the requirement of the SEEA implementation. The research results have, however, been important in developing both the methodology and estimates of the concerned measures for future implementation of the SEEA in India. As for illustration, the 'Natural Resources Accounting: A Framework for India' of the IGIDR (Parikh et al., 1993) proposed the assessment of physical environmental impacts of selected economic sectors and compilation of physical accounts for soil, air, water, forests, biodiversity and a number of non-renewable resources. Parikh and Parikh (1997) attempted to account for air pollution in India based on the input-output sectoral information at the all-India level using the 'Avoidance Cost' method of assessing the damage value due to air pollution.

Chopra and Kadekodi (1997), and Chopra et al. (2001), on the other hand, illustrate how to account for forests in the Yamuna Basin and all states in India, respectively. The methods used for the valuation of the forest-based goods and services included contingent valuation techniques (willingness to pay) and the Travel Cost method. Sankar (2004) also illustrates the valuation of environmental damage of industrial pollution in the leather industry. Sengupta and Mandal (2005) estimated the damage value of automotive air pollution in 35 urban agglomerations in India in terms of health cost and the monetized value of the health benefit if the emission standard were to conform to Euro norm IV. Kadekodi (2004), and Murty and Kumar (2004) cover a number of other illustrative case studies in the area of environmental valuation and impact assessment in India.

As building blocks for the ultimate construct of Integrated Environmental and Economic Accounting, special mention needs to be made of the works of Murty (2003), Haripriya (1998, 2000), GIST (2005), and TERI (1999), which have developed physical and monetary accounting for some environmental resource or economic sector. Murty (2003) developed both physical and monetary accounts of industrial water pollution and urban air pollution in India. He developed physical accounts of influent and effluent loads of BOD, COD and SS for the Indian water polluting industries for the years 1996–97 and 1997–98 based on some primary survey data. The corresponding monetary accounts of industrial water pollution, as developed, show the estimated adjusted NNP, corrected for the value of required reduction in industrial water pollution for sustainability to be 0.75 per cent lower than the conventional NNP figure.

In the case study of air pollution, Murty (2003) developed physical accounts of urban air pollution explaining the ambient concentration of SPM, NO_x and SO_2 for 15 major cities in India as well as monetary accounts providing a measure of damage valuation from urban air pollution at 0.66 per cent of the NNP in India.

In respect of Indian forest resources, Haripriya (1998) developed detailed forest accounts for the state of Maharashtra in both physical and monetary terms, incorporating species-wise production and prices, the extent of illegal logging, damage due to forest fires, insect infestation, and so forth. Her monetary accounts use the net price method to value the extent of logging, and to show the contribution of forests to SDP to be 3.6 per cent as opposed to the recorded 1.5 per cent in the conventional SNA-based State Accounts. However, it also shows that if the forest depletion were taken into account, the value added by the sector would drop by about 1 per cent of the SDP of the forestry sector. Haripriya (2000) extended further the accounts to incorporate the non-marketed products provided by the forests. The monetary account of such extension incorporated the pharmaceutical value of a hectare of biodiversity land derived by the use of the option value method.

The Green Indian States Trust (GIST) study on the 'Green Accounting for Indian States and Union Territories Project (GAISP)' has targeted to set up economic models for state-wise annual estimates of the Adjusted Gross

State Domestic Product in order to capture and analyze the true value addition at both the state and national levels by economic activities. The first monograph (GIST 2005) of this study incorporates forest resources into the National Accounts of India's States and Union Territories, using the satellite SEEA framework and accounts for timber, fuelwood, non-timber forest products and carbon sequestration effects for each state. The illustrative physical accounts for timber, fuelwood and carbon, and the overall depletion adjusted macroeconomic income for the Indian states are presented in Tables 10a to 10c.

A TERI (1999) study, entitled 'Natural resource accounting for the State of Goa', has developed depletion accounts for iron ore in Goa. The user-cost approach of valuation of depletion has yielded the adjusted NSDP from the mining sector to be 8–15 per cent lower than the conventional SNA-based estimates (see Table 11).

Similarly, the present authors estimated the resource rent and user cost-based depletion cost for the oil and natural gas sector in India for the period 1991–2003, as presented in Table 12. Such depletion accounting reduces the conventional SNA-based sectoral GDP estimate of the fuel mineral sector by 1–3 per cent.

17. Concluding Remarks

The development of the Economics of Natural Resources and the Environment has significantly contributed to the emergence of the concepts and methodology for measuring income, investment and other variables of macroeconomic identities, which conform to the notion of sustainability of development and human well-being. Extensive empirical research has taken place in the area of valuation of natural assets and regulatory policies for environmental control in the recent decades, and many important studies are ongoing in different countries. The problem of valuation, which involves the environmental impact assessment of economic activities, requires inter-disciplinary research as the socio-ecological dimensions of the problem of environmental conservation have to be addressed in such enquiries. While important data are being generated for the purpose of valuation and measurement of the natural environment through such research, more effort in this direction is required to get the results of estimates with higher reliability and robustness. However, the estimates of environmental valuation are likely to have a high degree of variance since the environmental valuation factors are specific to the socio-ecological context. As the environmental

GSDP, NSDP and ESDP for carbon for different states (million rupees) for 2002/03

State/ Union territory	GSDP	NSDP	Forestry and Logging	Adjusted NSDP	Depletion of timber and fuelwood	Depletion of carbon	Depletion of NTFPs	Total Depletion	ESDP	ESDP/ NSDP	Depletion of timber as % of NDP	Depletion of carbon as % of NDP	Depletion of NTFPs as % of NDP	Total Depletion % of NDP
Andhra Pradesh	1607683.90	1439753.90	16992.80	1453730.86	−8052.30	−7487.98	−2512.63	−8094.07	1445636.80	0.99	0.55	0.52	0.17	0.56
Bihar	897150.20	787033.60	23113.80	803573.95	−38730.49	−5103.13	−3288.86	−37809.55	765764.40	0.95	4.82	0.64	0.41	4.71
Goa	77711.20	67356.90	136.80	70863.76	506.03	327.53	8.22	327.53	71191.30	1.00	−0.71	−0.46	−0.01	−0.46
Gujarat	1382850.30	1144047.60	5307.50	1271916.72	−19026.96	−3924.00	−36.14	−4343.23	1267573.48	1.00	1.50	0.31	0.00	0.34
Haryana	658372.20	579374.90	1386.60	599546.21	−2826.12	−768.50	332.27	−2187.86	597359.35	1.00	0.47	0.13	−0.06	0.36
Himachal Pradesh	159460.00	142024.30	7198.80	141138.51	−4166.81	−155.19	1205.20	−2809.31	138529.19	0.98	2.95	0.11	−0.85	1.99
J & K	147495.90	128052.00	4653.90	133391.52	33560.89	1007.57	320.47	1007.57	134399.09	1.01	−25.16	−0.76	−0.24	−0.76
U.P.	1796014.70	1568624.70	21802.20	1628485.29	2138.29	−1272.74	297.42	−606.74	1627878.56	1.00	−0.13	0.08	−0.02	0.04
Karnataka	1139292.20	1004063.10	19120.90	1029435.50	12242.27	−938.32	362.336	698.00	1030133.50	1.00	−1.19	0.09	−0.04	−0.07
Kerala	761819.80	696021.20	13849.40	689093.27	−10820.43	−1743.70	−3183.68	−1943.65	687149.62	1.00	1.57	0.25	0.46	0.28
M.P.	1132756.60	974607.60	28846.70	1019420.99	7828.52	2472.62	−1952.87	3756.57	1023177.57	1.00	−0.77	−0.24	0.19	−0.37
Maharashtra	2951911.80	2632252.50	32471.10	2672291.73	4796.88	−4675.11	−2865.70	−3732.03	2668559.71	1.00	−0.18	0.17	0.11	0.14
Orissa	446844.50	387373.00	11326.90	402749.10	3783.55	−771.84	−936.40	570.51	403319.61	1.00	−0.94	0.19	0.23	−0.14
Punjab	707508.70	629677.50	2183.70	642935.52	−5652.58	−481.23	−254.29	−5700.36	637235.17	0.99	0.88	0.07	0.04	0.89
Rajasthan	873817.50	768878.00	11560.00	788085.83	−5542.89	−2465.67	−1086.50	−4956.45	783129.38	0.99	0.70	0.31	0.14	0.63
Sikkim	11527.30	10386.50	190.40	10407.554	−6447.23	309.86	62.16	−27.19	10380.35	1.00	61.95	−2.98	−0.60	0.26
Tamil Nadu	1537287.10	1367808.70	7177.20	1398966.56	−5760.97	−7781.77	−297.56	−7602.77	1391363.79	0.99	0.41	0.56	0.02	0.54
West Bengal	1671370.80	1537807.20	10498.20	1515621.63	−8878.11	−9907.43	−7078.81	−12015.19	1503606.44	0.99	0.59	0.65	0.47	0.79
A & N Island	11563.90	10407.51	64.60	10673.13	433.68	8229.93	−2.01	3616.88	14290.01	1.34	−4.06	−77.11	0.02	−33.89
Arunachal Pradesh	19450.50	17395.10	806.00	19092.20	45998.50	6134.84	−152.64	6134.84	25227.04	1.32	−240.93	−32.13	0.80	−32.13
Assam	354314.20	317208.00	5476.60	321714.02	7651.87	−747.18	−433.89	−747.18	320966.84	1.00	−2.38	0.23	0.13	0.23
Manipur	35312.60	32047.80	628.30	32473.47	−1378.26	−840.49	910.15	−565.00	31908.47	0.98	4.24	2.59	−2.80	1.74
Meghalaya	43429.20	38422.70	376.50	39927.60	−3237.09	−210.39	−245.92	−245.32	39682.28	0.99	8.11	0.53	0.62	0.61
Nagaland	36793.60	34272.00	1067.50	33308.47	10747.93	−965.48	−532.90	5994.94	39303.41	1.18	−32.27	2.90	1.60	−18.00
Tripura	60616.90	56603.40	762.10	55594.42	363.24	−2111.55	−943.19	−1921.26	53673.16	0.97	−0.65	3.80	1.70	3.46
Mizoram	17687.20	16346.10	167.20	16519.06	3899.09	−768.17	−463.83	634.15	17153.21	1.04	−23.60	4.65	2.81	−3.84
Total	18539942.80	16387845.81	227185.70	16801156.88	13322.05	−34617.3	−22766.57	−72549.05	16728607.83	1.00	−0.08	0.21	0.14	0.43

Source: GIST (2005).

TABLE 11

Monetary accounting of iron ore in Goa

Goa	1991	1992	1993	1994	1995	1996
Opening stock (000 tonnes)	816,600	814,480	812,355	810,222	808,066	805,923
Production (000 tonnes)	12,920	13,330	13,980	16,130	14,810	15,381
Closing stock (000 tonnes)	803,680	801150	798,375	794,092	793,256	790,542
Monetary accounting						
Production cost (Rs/tonne)	118	116	111	125	130	134
Pithead price (Rs/tonne)	279	236	281	255	296	324
Rent (net price) (Rs/tonne)	162	120	170	130	166	190
Total rent (Rs million)	2,087	1,596	2,373	210	2,458	2,926
Lifetime (years)	62	60	57	49	54	51
User cost method (Rs million)*	96	81	139	181	172	227
Conventional NSDP-mining (Rs million)	658	828	1601	1477	1714	1451
Adjusted NSDP mining (Rs million)	562	747	1462	1296	1542	1224

Source: TERI (1999), Report No. 99RD61.
Note: *user cost estimated at discount rate of 5 per cent.

and the socio-ecological and economic factors are sometimes inextricably combined in their reflection in data, more research is required to obtain the pure effect of environmental changes on economic assets and income.

The above observation is important for the standardization of the methods of estimation of the environmental impacts in physical and value terms for the different regions or countries, and for making them comparable after the purchasing power parity adjustment. Here, it may be commented that the comparability and standardization of environmental statistics would require greater dependence of the methods on market or technology-based objective factors than on subjective factors (like stated preferences) for the valuation of the environmental benefits or damages. The defensive/ maintenance cost approach would thus be preferable to the subjective willingness to pay approach for the valuation of environmental depreciation or environmental amenity services.

Finally, one may find that the implementation of the Natural Resource Accounting and the SEEA is often affected by political and economic considerations, while the plea is given in terms of lack of reliability of the database. The political lobbies of the different groups of business interests (like that of the energy industry—coal or oil) play a role in the progress of official funding of the required research and implementation of resource accounting in the National Accounts. This further emphasizes the need for intensive and extensive research in the area, and greater exchange and sharing of research results and data in the interest of standardization and comparability.

TABLE 12

Physical and monetary accounts of oil and natural gas reserves in India

Year	Recoverable reserves: opening stock* (MMT)	Production (MMT)	Reserves: revaluation (MMT)	Recoverable reserves: closing stock (MMT)	Life span of recoverable reserves (years)	Total rent at 10% RoR (Rs in crores) Current prices	User cost at discount rate=10% (Rs in crores) Current prices	Conventional fuel mineral GDP (Rs in crores) Current prices	Adjusted fuel mineral GDP (Rs in crores) Current prices	Adjusted fuel mineral GDP as % of Conventional fuel mineral GDP
	a	b	c (= d – a + b)	d	e (= a/b)	f	g	h	i (= h – g)	j (= i/h*100)
1990–91	1463	49	49	1463	29.7	6,227	333	11,430	11,097	97.1%
1991–92	1463	47	9	1425	31	3,520	166	12,098	11,932	98.6%
1992–93	1425	43	19	1401	33	4,628	181	14,000	13,819	98.7%
1993–94	1401	44	–17	1341	32.2	3,809	161	16,538	16,377	99.0%
1994–95	1341	50	17	1308	27	3,694	257	18,546	18,289	98.6%
1995–96	1308	56	118	1370	23.5	3,288	317	20,264	19,947	98.4%
1996–97	1370	54	8	1324	25.4	3,044	245	22,703	22,458	98.9%
1997–98	1324	58	–41	1226	23	3,594	366	27,510	27,144	98.7%
1998–99	1226	57	218	1387	21.3	5,413	643	28,935	28,292	97.8%
1999–2000	1387	58	90	1419	24.1	6,055	554	33,802	33,248	98.4%
2000–01	1419	59	57	1417	24.1	10,196	935	37,275	36,340	97.5%
2001–02	1417	59	171	1530	24.1	10,633	971	39,248	38,277	97.5%
2002–03	1530	61	101	1570	25	21,328	1,797	52,057	50,260	96.5%
2003–04	1570	62	269	1777	25.3	15,568	1,274	53,787	52,513	97.6%

Source: Authors' own calculations.

Note: *All figures pertain to reserves and production of oil and natural gas combined (in terms of oil equivalent).

All these arguments also provide a case for awarding greater priority to the support for environmental economic research on resource accounting and adjustment of the National Accounts System in India. At the present stage of data development, it would be prudent to make gradual progress towards the implementation of the SEEA in India. It is important to initiate now the development of physical asset accounts for important produced and non-produced environmental assets, and physical material flow account and hybrid flow account for the development of environmental and resource use policies. The extent of coverage of monetization in the total scope of the physical asset and flow accounts should depend on the stage of development of the database, and on the standardization of the method of valuation of environmental resources and the robustness of the results of valuation. The UN System of Integration of Environmental and Economic Accounting has, in fact, cautioned against immediate variation of the production boundary to include environmental services. The environmental adjustments of the macroeconomic aggregates may be attempted by stages, beginning by adjustments for only such items of depletion or degradation for which reliable physical data and monetary valuation are available. These value adjustments can cover increasingly more items of environmental changes as and when the database of physical and monetary accounts develops further. The development of reliable hybrid flow accounts and asset accounts is more important than unreliable estimates of environmentally adjusted macro-aggregates for analyzing the environmental consequences of a pattern of growth and development, and for developing policy models. Greater thrust on development and regular updating of the environmental database and on the inter-disciplinary research on environmental valuation would, however, be important for ensuring quick progress towards implementation of the progressively advanced versions of the SEEA, as discussed in the preceding section. The ultimate full implementation of the integrated environmental and economic accounting is, however, crucial for analyzing the macroeconomic aspects of the environmental changes and for the development of sustainable macroeconomic development policies.

Ramprasad Sengupta, Centre for Economic Studies and Planning, School of Social Sciences, Jawaharlal Nehru University, New Delhi 110067, India. E-mail: rps0302@gmail.com

Shalini Saksena, Delhi College of Arts and Commerce, University of Delhi, New Delhi 110023, India. E-mail: saksena.shalini@gmail.com

References

Ayres, R.U. 1978. *Resources, Environment, and Economics: Applications of the Materials/ Energy Balance Principle*. New York: John Wiley and Sons.

Ayres, R.U. and A.V. Kneese. 1969. 'Production, Consumption and Externalities', *American Economic Review,* 59(3): 282–97.

CBS (Statistics Netherlands). 2006. *Present Status and Future Developments of the Dutch NAMEA*, Statistics Netherlands, Voorburg, Paper for the International Workshop for Interactive Analysis on Economy and Environment, 4 March, Tokyo.

Central Statistical Organization. 1997, 2003, 2006. *Compendium of Environmental Statistics*, Department of Statistics, Ministry of Planning and Programme Implementation, New Delhi: Government of India.

Chopra, K. and G. Kadekodi. 1997. 'Natural Resource Accounting in Yamuna Basin: Accounting for Forest Resources', (monograph), New Delhi: Institute of Economic Growth.

Chopra, K., B.B. Bhattacharya and P. Kumar. 2001. 'Contribution of Forestry Sector to Gross Domestic Product in India', Draft, New Delhi: Institute of Economic Growth, . Project Sponsored by the Ministry of Environment and Forests, Government of India.

Cumberland, J.H. 1966. 'A Regional Inter-industry Model for Analysis of Development Objectives', *Papers and Proceedings of the Regional Science Association*, 17: 61–75.

Daly, H.E. 1968. 'On Economics as a Life Science', *Journal of Political Economy,* 76(3):392–406.

Daly, H.E. and J. Farley. 2003. *Ecological Economics: Principles and Application*, Washington: Island Press.

Dasgupta, P. 2001. *Human Well-being and the Natural Environment*. New Delhi: Oxford University Press.

Dasgupta, P. and K.G. Mäler. 2000. 'Net National Product, Wealth, and Social Well-being', *Environment and Development Economics*, 5(1): 69–93.

Dasgupta, S. and T. Mitra, 2001. 'National Product, Income Accounts and Sustainable Development' in A. Bose, D. Ray and A. Sarkar (eds), *Contemporary Macroeconomics*.New Delhi: Oxford University Press.

El Serafy, S. 1991.'The Proper Calculation of Income from Depletable Natural Resources', in Y.J. Ahmed, S. El Serafy and Ernst Lutz (eds), *Environmental Accounting for Sustainable Development*. Washington, D.C.: UNEP, World Bank Symposium.

Federal Statistical Office Germany. 2006. 'The German System of Environmental–Economic Accounting Concept, Current State and Application', Paper Presented at the Workshop on 'Rationale and Methods for Measuring Environmental Impact', 18–19 September, New Delhi.

GIST. 2005. 'The Value of Timber, Carbon, Fuelwood, and Non-timber Forest Products in India's Forests', Monograph 1 of the Green Accounting for Indian States Project, Green Indian States Trust.

Hamilton, K. and G. Ruta. 2006. 'From Curse to Blessing: Natural Resources and Institutional Quality', *Environment Matters 2006*, Annual Review:24–7.

Hamilton, K. and M. Clemens. 1999. 'Genuine Savings Rates in Developing Countries', *The World Bank Economic Review*, 13(2):333–56.

Haripriya, G.S. 1998. 'Forest Resource Accounting for the State of Maharashtra in India', *Development Policy Review*, 16 (2): 131–151.

———. 2000. 'Integrating Forest Resources into the System of National Accounts in Maharashtra', *Environment and Development Economics*, 5(1): 143–56.

Hartwick, J. 1977. 'Inter-generational Equity and Investing of Rents from Exhaustible Resources', *American Economic Review*, 66: 972–74.

Hartwick, J. and A. Hageman. 1993. 'Economic Depreciation of Mineral Stocks and the Contribution of El Serafy', in Ernst Lutz (ed.), *Toward Improved Accounting for the Environment*, 211–235. Washington, D.C.: The World Bank.

Hicks, J. R. 1946. *Value and Capital*. Oxford: Oxford University Press.

Hotelling, H. 1931. 'The Economics of Exhaustible Resources', *Journal of Political Economy*, 39(2):137–75.

Isard, W., K. Bassett, C. Choguill, J. Furtado, R. Izumita, J. Kissin, E. Romanoff, R. Seyfarth and R. Tatlock. 1967. 'On the Linkage of Socio-economic and Ecologic Systems', *Papers and Proceedings of the Regional Science Association*, 21: 79–99.

Kadekodi, G. (ed.). 2004. *Environmental Economics in Practice*. New Delhi: Oxford University Press.

Leontief, W. 1970.'Environmental Repercussions and the Economic Structure: An Input-Output Approach', *The Review of Economics and Statistics*, 52(3): 262–71.

Mäler, K.G. 1991. 'National Accounts and Environmental Resources', *Environmental and Resource Economics*, 1: 1–15.

Murty, M.N. 2003.'Measuring Environmentally Corrected Net National Product: Case Studies of Industrial Water Pollution and Urban Air Pollution in India', mimeo, Delhi: Institute of Economic Growth.

Murty, M.N. and S. Kumar. 2004. *Environmental and Economic Accounting for Industry*. New Delhi: Oxford University Press.

Parikh, K.S. and J. Parikh. 1997. *Accounting and Valuation of the Environment*. Vol. 1: A Premier for Developing Countries, Vol. 2: Case Studies from ESCAP Region. New York: United Nations.

Parikh, K.S., J.K. Parikh, V.K. Sharma and J.P. Painuly. 1993. 'Natural Resource Accounting—A Framework for India', Indira Gandhi Institute of Development Research, Report Prepared for the Ministry of Environment and Forests. New Delhi: Government of India.

Perman, R., Yue Ma and G. James. Mc. 1996. *Natural Resource and Environmental Economics*, Chapter 13. England: Addison Wesley Longman Limited.

Pearson, D. 1989. *The Natural House Book*. New York: Simon and Schuster, Inc.

Sankar, U. 2004.'Pollution Control in Tanneries', in G. Kadekodi (eds), *Environmental Economics in Practice*. New Delhi: Oxford University Press.

Sengupta, R. and S. Mandal. 2005. 'Health Damage Cost of Automotive Air Pollution: Cost Benefit Analysis of Fuel Quality Upgradation for Indian Cities', National Institute of Public Finance and Policy, Working Paper No. 37, New Delhi.

Statistics Canada. 2000. *E-connections: Linking the Environment and the Economy: Indicators and Detailed Statistics*. STC 16–200–XKE.

TERI. 1999. Pilot Project on Natural Resource Accounting in Goa (Phase I), Prepared for Directorate of Planning and Statistics, Goa, Tata Energy Research Institute Project Report No. 99RD61.

UNSD. 1993. *Integrated Environmental and National Accounting*. Interim Version, Handbook of National Accounting, Series F, No.61, Department of Economic and Social Development. New York: United Nations Statistical Division.

———. 2000. *Integrated Environmental and Economic Accounting: An Operational Manual*. Handbook of National Accounting, Series F, No.78.

———. 2003. *Integrated Environmental and Economic Accounting: An Operational Manual*, Handbook of National Accounting.

Victor, P. A. 1972. *Pollution: Economy and Environment*. London: George Allen and Unwin Ltd.

Weitzman, M. 1976. 'On the Welfare Significance of National Product in a Dynamic Economy', *Quarterly Journal of Economics*, 90 (1): 156–162.

World Bank. 1999. *World Development Indicators*. Washington, DC: The World Bank.

———. 2006. 'Where is the Wealth of Nations? Measuring Capital for the Twenty-first Century', Available online at http://go.worldbank.org/2QTH26ULQ0.7

Liberalization of Government Procurements: Welfare Effects of Foreign Entry

Ngo Van Long*
Department of Economics, McGill University, Montréal,
Québec, Canada

The recent trend of trade liberalization has resulted in increased international pressure on governments to allow foreign bidders for government contracts. In this article, the welfare effects of relaxing government restrictions on bidding by foreign firms are analyzed, using a modified version of the Tullock model of rent contests. It is shown that opening the bidding to foreign firms can, under certain conditions, improve social welfare of the liberalizing country, even when the foreign firms are less efficient in production than some domestic firms. The gain partly comes from reduced aggregate domestic lobbying effort, even though foreign firms also lobby.

JEL Classification: F10
Keywords: Trade liberalization, Contest, Lobbying, Welfare

1. Introduction

In many countries, government procurements are typically reserved for domestic firms. The recent trend of trade liberalization has resulted in increased international pressure on governments to 'open up' the list of potential bidders for government contracts. Foreign firms are becoming

* I would like to thank Eric Bond, Kim Long, Sugata Marjit, and participants at the International Conference on International Trade (Kolkata, January 2006) for comments on an earlier version of this paper. Supports from SSHRC and FQRCS are gratefully acknowledged.

eligible to bid for government contracts in a wide range of economic activities, ranging from road and bridge construction to developing and running a casino complex (sometimes called 'integrated resorts facilities'). An interesting question arises: Does the removal of restrictions on foreign firms' participation in government procurements lead to an increase in domestic welfare?

The answer to the above question depends on the mechanism by which government officials choose the winner. Quite often, governments declare from the outset that the contract is not necessarily awarded to the highest bidder because there are other relevant dimensions that are not easily quantifiable. These include concerns such as whether a bidder has sufficient financial resources or expertise to carry out the project, whether it has a good safety record, or whether there is some shadow of doubt about its possible links with organized crimes, and so forth. Governments typically do not specify the formula and weights by which all relevant dimensions of a bid are assessed. Even when the identities of the bidders are public knowledge, it is quite difficult to predict who the winner will be. (The announcement made in Singapore in June 2005 by the selection committee for the 2012 Olympics site, that London is the winner, is a striking example of how difficult it can be to predict the votes of officials.)

In this article, we analyze the welfare effects of relaxing government restrictions on bidding by foreign firms, using a modified version of the Tullock model of rent contests (Tullock 1980; Rowley et al. 1988; Nitzan 1994). Tullock assumes that the probability of any given agent winning a rent-seeking contest depends on the ratio of his own effort to the sum of the efforts expended by all agents. In his model, agents are homogeneous: they have equal valuations of the prize, and their efforts have equal effectiveness. We relax these assumptions and introduce heterogeneity in both: (*i*) valuations of the prize and (*ii*) comparative advantage in lobbying, in order to capture more adequately the real world features of rent-seeking, in the context of government procurements in particular. The rent associated with winning a procurement contract depends on the firm's production cost. If foreign firms have lower production costs than domestic firms, their valuations of the 'prize' will be higher. On the other hand, the rent-seeking efforts of foreign firms may not be as effective as those of domestic firms, because the latter group is better informed about the channels by which a government's decisions can be influenced. In this article, we develop an index of comparative disadvantage in lobbying and model liberalization as a decrease in this index for foreign firms.

The evaluation of social welfare gain for a liberalizing country is complicated and should take into account several factors. First, while the profit of foreign firms should not be counted in social welfare, if a domestic bidder wins, its after-tax rent should be included as part of the welfare gain. Second, while all the resource costs in rent-seeking by domestic firms should be subtracted from the social welfare, in contrast, the resource costs in rent-seeking incurred by foreign firms are not part of the social cost. This is because the foreign firms either use foreign resources, or hire domestic resources, whose earnings should be considered as export revenue. Third, when a foreign firm is allowed to bid for government procurements, this will change the equilibrium lobbying effort levels of all domestic firms: some domestic firms will intensify their lobbying activities, while other domestic firms will scale them down. Finally, the probability of a given firm winning will be affected by adjustments in the lobbying intensities of all firms.

In this article, we show that opening the bidding to foreign firms can, under certain conditions, improve the social welfare of the liberalizing country, even when the foreign firms are less efficient in production than some domestic firms. The gain partly comes from a reduced aggregate domestic lobbying effort, even though foreign firms also lobby.

In our model, rents are partially dissipated by contests for rents. Dissipation is not complete because each contestant has some power: it can influence the probability of winning of other firms. Even though there is free entry, equilibrium is not determined by zero rent of the marginal firm: under the assumption of a discrete distribution of firm types, with a finite number of firms of each type, the intra-marginal firms enjoy positive rents. The lobbying efforts by domestic firms constitute a social waste: resources are used in an attempt to transfer money from one person's pocket to another's. The enjoyment of power by the bureaucrats is assumed to be exogenous, and is not counted as part of social welfare. (It can, of course, be argued that the 'ego rents' earned by bureaucrats are endogenous and any changes in ego rents should be counted in the cost-benefit calculus; we do not follow that approach.)

2. The Model

For concreteness, consider a government which wants to establish a casino complex with the aim of attracting a specified flow T of foreign tourists that would result in increased employment of the home country's unskilled workers. We assume that the government does not require firms to submit bids in monetary value, and that, instead, each candidate firm must submit a plan of how the site will be developed and operated. Government officials will choose as winner, the firm whose submitted development-cum-operation plan is judged to be most likely to achieve the targeted tourist flow T. The winning firm's obligation is to develop and operate the site according to its winning plan, and to pay profit tax at the exogenous rate t per dollar of profit. We assume that the actual profit is observable and verifiable by government officials once the firm starts its operation.

Following Tullock (1980) and Hillman and Riley (1989), we do not explicitly model how government officials make their decision, and simply specify that any candidate firm which undertakes some lobbying effort has a positive chance of winning the contract. Hillman and Riley refer to this model as an 'imperfectly discriminating contests' model. We assume that before (and even at) the time when the winner is announced, government officials have no knowledge of the potential profitability of any firm. On the other hand, we assume at the lobbying stage, that each firm i has perfect knowledge of its own profitability, and knows the lobbying strategies of its rivals. Government officials receive 'documents' (sent by the firms) which supposedly influence their perception of the relative merits of the plans of the candidate firms. We assume that these documents have no social values, that is, they have no valuable information contents. (Thus, we are not modelling the rent-seeking game as a signalling game.)

In our welfare calculation, we do not count the enjoyment of power by government officials. The 'ego rents' earned by officials when they receive and evaluate documents are not counted in social welfare; this is in keeping with the tradition that envy should not be counted in cost-benefit analysis.

2.1 Domestic Firms, Foreign Firms, and Domestic Welfare

Suppose there are two groups of firms which are permitted to bid for government procurements: m_d domestic firms and m_f foreign firms. Let D denote the set of domestic firms, and F, the set of foreign firms. Let $m = m_d + m_f$. We assume that $m > 2$, and $m_d \geq 2$, so that there are at least two potential domestic rent-seekers.

Let M be the union of the two sets D and F. It is the set of all potential rent-seekers in the game. After evaluations of 'documents' by bureaucrats, one firm will be selected as the winner. (This is a winner-takes-all game.) The probability of firm i winning is assumed to be:

$$p_i = \frac{s_i / \beta_i}{\sum s_j / \beta_j} \tag{1}$$

where s_i is firm i's expenditure on lobbying (which includes preparation of documents, formal and informal meetings, etc.) and β_i is the (exogenous) effectiveness parameter of its lobbying expenditure. If the contract (often called 'prize' in rent-seeking literature) is awarded to firm i, it generates a profit flow R_i. Let t be the tax rate on profit. Each firm takes the lobbying expenditure of other firms as given, and chooses s_i to maximize its expected net gain:

$$\pi_i = \frac{s_i / \beta_i}{\sum s_j / \beta_j} tR - s_i \tag{2}$$

A Nash equilibrium of the game is a strategy profile such that for each firm i, the strategy s_i is its best response to the strategies of the other firms.

Formally, the outcome of the game is the assignment to each firm i a probability p_i that it will be the winner. From the home country's point of view, social welfare, denoted by W, is the sum of: (a) expected government revenue and (b) domestic firms' expected net gains. In this social welfare expression, the foreign contribution is only through tax revenue. Notice that for domestic firms, the lobbying cost is subtracted from social welfare, because we assume that the costs are real resource costs, not money transfers (such as bribes). For example, if a domestic firm hires a lobbyist to prepare and transmit a document, the lobbyist's time is withdrawn from socially useful activities (production of intermediate or final goods) and re-allocated to socially useless rent-contest activities (transferring money from one pocket to another.)

2.2 A Transformation of Variables

It is convenient to transform variables by defining the 'effective effort' of player i as:

$$g_i = s_i / \beta_i \tag{3}$$

Then β_i may be interpreted as player i's cost (in money terms) of achieving one unit of g_i. Define 'aggregate effective effort' as the sum of the effective efforts of all rent-seekers:

$$G = \sum_{j \in M} g_j \tag{4}$$

Define G_{-i} to be the sum of efforts of firm i's rivals.
Then the probability of success of firm i is:

$$p_i = \frac{g_i}{g_i + G_{-i}} \tag{5}$$

For given G_{-i}, firm i's problem 1 is now transformed into the following format: choose g_i to maximize

$$\pi_i \equiv \beta_i F_i(g_i) \equiv \beta_i \left[\frac{g_i}{G_{-i} + g_i} \left(\frac{(1-t)R_i}{\beta_i} \right) - g_i \right] \tag{6}$$

We call $F_i(g_i)$ the surrogate profit of firm i. It differs from π_i by the factor β_i. It is convenient to define

$$v_1 = \frac{(1-t)R_i}{\beta_i} \tag{7}$$

and call v_i player i's 'effective valuation'.

Without loss of generality, we order players so that

$$v_1 \geq v_2 \geq v_3 ... \geq v_m > 0$$

It is also useful to define

$$y_i = \frac{1}{v_i} \tag{8}$$

We will refer to y_i as agent i's 'comparative disadvantage in lobbying'.

Assumption 1: (Foreign firms have strong comparative disadvantage in lobbying.) *Before liberalization, foreign firms have strong comparative disadvantage in lobbying. In the list of m firms that are ordered in terms of comparative disadvantage in lobbying, the first m_d firms are domestic firms, and the remaining firms are foreign firms.*

Let us define, for any positive integer $k \leq m$, the sum of the comparative disadvantage levels of the first k firms as:

$$Y_k \equiv \sum_{i=1}^{k} y_i \tag{9}$$

Assumption 1 implies that

$$my_m \geq Y_m \tag{10}$$

Assumption 2: (There is strong heterogeneity of comparative disadvantage in lobbying.) The following inequality holds:

$$(m-1)y_m \geq Y_m \tag{11}$$

As will be seen below, this assumption implies that firm m, the foreign firm with the greatest comparative disadvantage level, will not be an active rent-seeker. (Note that our specification that $m>2$ ensures that Assumption 2 can be satisfied.)

Firm i takes G_{-i} as given and chooses g_i to maximize its expected profit. In what follows, we assume that $G_{-i} >0$.

Let us note the following properties of the function $F_i(g_i)$:

(*i*)   For any given $G_{-i} > 0$, $F_i(g_i)$ is zero at $g_i = 0$.
(*ii*) $F_i'(0)$ is positive if, and only if,

$$v_i > G_{-i} \tag{12}$$

(*iii*) It can easily be verified that the function $F_i(g_i)$ is strictly concave, and that its derivative is negative if g_i is sufficiently large.

From the above observations, we obtain the following result:

Result 1: Given $G_{-i} > 0$, the maximization problem of firm i has a unique solution. A firm will choose to be active in lobbying if, and only if, the sum of the effective efforts of its rivals is strictly less than its own valuation of the prize. It follows that if $G_{-i} \geq v_i$, then $g_i = 0$, otherwise,

$$g_i = \sqrt{G_{-i}v_i} - G_{-i} > 0 \tag{13}$$

2.3 Properties of Nash Equilibrium of the Lobbying Game

We say that agent i is an active rent-seeker if his equilibrium lobbying effort is strictly positive.

Result 2: In a Nash equilibrium, there are at least two active rent-seekers.

Proof: Suppose there were a Nash equilibrium wherein player i is the only active rent-seeker. Then $G_{-i} = 0$, and player i would choose $g_i = 0$ but this would make $F_j'(0)$ equal infinity. So player j would choose a strictly positive effort level, contradicting $G_{-j} = 0$.

Consider a Nash equilibrium in which n rent-seekers are active. Let A denote the set of active rent-seekers in that Nash equilibrium. Let us define

$$Y_A \equiv \sum_{i \in A} y_i \tag{14}$$

$$G_A \equiv \sum_{i \in A} g_i \tag{15}$$

Then, for all $i \in A$, the following FOC holds:

$$G_A^2 = [G_A - g_i] v_i \tag{16}$$

Thus, the following equation holds in equilibrium, for all $i \in A$:

$$g_i = G_A \left[1 - \frac{G_A}{v_i} \right] \tag{17}$$

Summing over all $i \in A$:

$$G_A = n G_A - Y_A (G_A)^2 \tag{18}$$

where n is the number of elements of set A, that is, the number of active rent-seekers in the Nash equilibrium, and Y_A is the sum of the comparative disadvantage indices of all active rent-seekers.

Dividing by G_A, we get:

$$1 = n - Y_A(G_A) \tag{19}$$

Definition 1: *The 'modified average comparative disadvantage in lobbying' of a group of firms A that consists of n firms is: $Y_A/(n-1)$*

We obtain the following result:

Proposition 1: *In a Nash equilibrium with n active rent-seekers, their aggregate effective lobbying effort is equal to the inverse of their modified average comparative disadvantage in lobbying:*

$$G_A = \frac{n-1}{Y_A} \tag{20}$$

Remark: This proposition is equivalent to the Hillman–Riley result that 'total outlays closely approximate the harmonic mean of individuals' valuations as the number of participants increases'.

We now turn to the question of uniqueness of the Nash equilibrium. We will show below that the Nash equilibrium is unique for our general formulation. Before doing so, we must establish a few results.

Result 3: *Let A be the set of active firms in a Nash equilibrium. If firm $i \in A$, then any firm j with $y_j \leq y_i$ also belongs to A.*

Corollary: *If there are exactly n active firms in a Nash equilibrium, they must be the first n firms in the list.*

It follows that $A = \{1,2,3,...,n\}$ and $Y_A = Y_n$.

Result 4: Under Assumption 2, there exists a unique integer $n \in \{2,3,...,m-1\}$ such that

$$y_n < \frac{Y_n}{n-1} \tag{21}$$

$$y_{n+1} \geq \frac{Y_n}{n-1} \tag{22}$$

Proposition 2 (Uniqueness of the Nash Equilibrium) *Let M be the set of permitted rent-seekers. Given Assumption 2, only $n < m$ rent-seekers are active, where n is uniquely determined by the two inequalities in Result 4 above. Their equilibrium aggregate effective effort in lobbying is equal to*

$$G_A = \frac{n-1}{Y_A} \tag{23}$$

And the equilibrium pure strategies of players are as follows. For $i < n$

$$g_i = G(1-Gy_i) = \left(\frac{n-1}{Y_n}\right)\left[1-\frac{(n-1)y_i}{Y_n}\right] \tag{24}$$

where Y_n satisfies the cut-off condition

$$y_{n+1} \geq \frac{Y_n}{n-1} > y_n \tag{25}$$

For $i > n$, $g_i = 0$, that is, the players do not lobby.

Proof: The uniqueness of the set of active firms follows from Result 4. To show the uniqueness of the strategies, let us suppose there are two different equilibrium strategy profiles, $g = \{g_1, g_2, ..., g_n, 0, 0, 0..., 0\}$ and $q = \{q_1, q_2, ..., q_n, 0, 0, 0..., 0\}$. Then, for all $i \in \{1, 2, ..., n\}$,

$$\frac{G - g_i}{Q - q_i} = \frac{G^2}{Q^2} \equiv \omega \tag{26}$$

Thus, for all $i \in \{1, 2, ..., n\}$,

$$(Q - q_i)\omega = G - g_i. \tag{27}$$

Summing over all active firms:

$$(n-1)Q\omega = (n-1)G \tag{28}$$

Thus:

$$(n-1)Q\frac{Q^2}{G^2} \equiv (n-1)G \tag{29}$$

Hence $Q = G$ and thus $q_i = g_i$.

3. Properties of Equilibrium Strategies

Proposition 3: *For any active firm i, the following properties hold:*
(i) **(Monotonicity of lobbying effort in own comparative advantage)** *Suppose y_i increases by a small amount (while all other y_j stay unchanged), such that n remains unchanged and the cut-off condition remains valid at n. The firm which suffers an increase in its index y_i will reduce its equilibrium lobbying effort.*
(ii) **(Non-monotonicity of lobbying effort in rival's comparative advantage)** *Suppose for some $j < n$, where $j \neq i$, y_i increases by a small amount, such that n remains unchanged and the cut-off condition remains valid at n. Then firm i will decrease its lobbying effort if, and only if,*

$$y_i < \frac{y_n}{2(n-1)} \tag{30}$$

Proof: Omitted.

4. Entry of a Foreign Firm

Suppose, initially, there are n active domestic players, and all foreign firms are inactive because their β_f are too high. We let

$$Y_n^d \equiv \sum_{i=1}^n y_i^d \tag{31}$$

Here, the superscript d is used to remind us that the sum is over n domestic firms. Then:

$$Y_{n+1}^d \geq \frac{Y_n^d}{n-1} > Y_n^d \tag{32}$$

and the equilibrium total contribution is, from Proposition 1:

$$G = \frac{n-1}{Y_n^d} \tag{33}$$

Suppose now a foreign firm f experiences a sufficiently big fall in its beta, so that y^f falls below the threshold level, that is,

$$y^f < \frac{Y_n^d}{n-1} \tag{34}$$

This inequality implies

$$ny^f < Y_n^d + y^f \tag{35}$$

There are two cases to be considered.

Case A: The foreign firm's comparative disadvantage in lobbying, while satisfying the condition that it is below the threshold level, is still at least as great as that of the most lobby-inefficient domestic firm, that is,

$$y^f \geq y_n^d \tag{36}$$

so that at the new equilibrium, there are n+1 active rent-seekers.

Case B: The foreign firm's comparative disadvantage in lobbying is lower than that of a non-empty subset of domestic firms, so that n–k domestic firms cease to be active. In this case

$$\gamma_{k+i}^d \geq \frac{\gamma_1^d + \ldots + \gamma_k^d + \gamma^f}{k} \qquad (37)$$

while

$$\gamma^f < \frac{\gamma_1^d + \ldots + \gamma_k^d + \gamma^f}{k} \qquad (38)$$

Example 1: (Case A) Initially, n=3 with $\gamma_1^d = 1$, $\gamma_2^d = 2$ and $\gamma_3^d = 2.4$. Then

$$\gamma_3^d < \frac{1+2+2.4}{n-1} = 2.7 \qquad (39)$$

Now, after the fall in β^f, let $\gamma^f = 2.4$. At the new equilibrium, all the four firms are active, since

$$\gamma_3^d = \gamma^f < \frac{1+2+2.4+2.4}{4-1} = 2.6 \qquad (40)$$

Example 2: (Case B) Initially, $n=3$ with $\gamma_1^d = 1$, $\gamma_2^d = 2$ and $\gamma_3^d = 2.4$. After the fall in β^f, let $\gamma^f = 1.5$. Then the domestic firm 3 ceases to be active because

$$\gamma_3^d > \frac{1+1.5+2}{2} = 2.25 \qquad (41)$$

Proposition 4: *In both cases A and B, total effective lobbying effort increases after the entry.*
Proof: Consider, first, Case B. Before entry, there are n active firms. After entry, there are $n-(n-k)+1=k+1$ active firms, of which k domestic firms. Let G^b and G^a denote the pre-entry and post-entry aggregate efforts. We will show that $G^a > G^b$. This holds if, and only if,

$$\frac{k}{Y_k^d + \gamma^f} > \frac{n-1}{Y_n^d} \qquad (42)$$

that is, if, and only if,

$$kY_n^d > (n-1)\left(Y_k^d + y^f\right). \tag{43}$$

Now consider the left-hand side of the above inequality:

$$kY_k^d \equiv kY_k^d + k\left(y_{k+1}^d + \dots + y_n^d\right) \geq kY_k^d + (n-k)ky_{k+1}^d \geq kY_k^d + (n-k)\left(Y_k^d + y^f\right) \tag{44}$$

$$= nY_k^d + (n-k)y^f > (n-1)Y_k^d + (n-1)\left(y^f\right)$$

where the last strict inequality follows from

$$y^f < \frac{Y_k^d + y^f}{k} \tag{45}$$

It follows that $kY_n^d > (n-1)(Y_k^d + y^f)$.

Next, consider Case A. Simply set $k = n$ and the above proof applies to this case.

Proposition 5: (Entry of a foreign firm leads to decreased lobbying by inefficient domestic firms.) *Suppose that before entry, there are n active firms. The (before entry) equilibrium lobbying effort of domestic firm i is, for i<n,*

$$g_i^b = G^b\left(1 - G y_i^d\right) = \frac{n-1}{Y_n^d}\left[1 - \left(\frac{n-1}{Y_n^d}\right)y_i^d\right] \equiv X^b\left(1 - X^b y_i^d\right) \tag{46}$$

After entry, there are k+1 active firms, where k=n in case A and k<n in case B. The (after entry) equilibrium lobbying effort of domestic firm i is, for i ≤ k,

$$g_i^a = G^a\left(1 - G^a y_i^d\right) = \frac{k}{Y_k^d + y^f}\left[1 - \left(\frac{k}{Y_n^k + y^f}\right)y_i^d\right] \equiv X^a\left(1 - X^a y_i^d\right) \tag{47}$$

There exists a critical level of y, denoted by y_c, such that domestic firm will intensify its lobbying effort upon the entry of the foreign firm if and only if $y_i^d < y_c$.

Proof: Define

$$Y^a \equiv Y_k^d + y^f \tag{48}$$

We want to find a value y_c such that if $y^d_i < y_c$ then:

$$\frac{g^b_i}{g^a_i} < 1 \tag{49}$$

Now:

$$\frac{g^b_i}{g^a_i} = \frac{X^b\left(1 - X^b y^d_i\right)}{X^a\left(1 - X^a y^d_i\right)} \tag{50}$$

Hence, $g^b_i < g^a_i$ if, and only if, the following critical inequality is satisfied:

$$y^d_i\left(X^a + X^b\right)\left(X^a - X^b\right) < X^a - X^b \tag{51}$$

Note that:

$$X^a - X^b = \frac{k}{Y^a} - \frac{n-1}{Y^d_n} > 0$$

$$X^a + X^b = \frac{(2n-1)Y^d_n + (n-1)y^f}{Y^a Y^d_n} > 0$$

It follows that the above critical inequality is satisfied if, and only if,

$$y^d_i < \frac{1}{X^b + X^a} \equiv y_c \tag{52}$$

Example 3: There are two domestic firms, with $y^d_1 = 0.10$ and $y^d_2 = 0.20$. Firm 3, the foreign firm, has a high comparative disadvantage before liberalization, say $y^f_3 = 4/10$. Then, before liberalization, only two of the three domestic firms are active:

$$Y^b_n < \frac{1}{10} + \frac{1}{5} = \frac{3}{10} \tag{53}$$

$$G^b = \frac{n-1}{Y_n} = 3.333 \tag{54}$$

$$g_1^b = G^b\left(1 - G^b y_1^d\right) = 2.222$$

$$g_2^b = G^b\left(1 - G^b y_2^d\right) = 1.111$$

After liberalization, suppose β^f falls so that $y_3^f = 1/5 = y_2^d$. Then entry for the foreign firm is profitable. After entry,

$$Y_{n+1}^a = \frac{1}{10} + \frac{1}{5} + \frac{1}{5} = \frac{1}{2}$$

It follows that:

$$Y_c = \frac{1}{X^b + X^a} = \frac{Y_n^b Y_{n+1}^a}{(2n-1)Y_n^b + (n-1)y^f} = 0.11538 \tag{55}$$

Thus, $G^a = 4$, $g_1^a = 2.43 > g_1^b$ and $g_3^a = g_2^a = 0.8 < g_2^b$.

Remark: This example shows that the sum of the lobbying efforts of the two domestic firms falls after the foreign entry.

We now state a necessary and sufficient condition for aggregate domestic lobbying to fall.

Aggregate domestic lobbying falls if, and only if,

$$G^a - g^f - G^b < 0$$

Now:

$$g^f = G^a - y^f (G^a)^2$$

Thus the necessary and sufficient condition is:

$$y^f (G^a)^2 - G^b < 0 \tag{56}$$

That is,

$$y^f < \left(\frac{n-1}{Y_n^b}\right)\left(\frac{Y_k + y^f}{k}\right)^2 \tag{57}$$

This inequality is satisfied if y^f is close to zero.

Proposition 6: *If the foreign entrant is very efficient, the total aggregate domestic lobbying effort will fall (but will remain positive).*

Proof: Omitted.

5. Effects of Foreign Entry on Welfare

Consider two scenarios. In the first scenario, all rent-seekers are domestic firms. The foreign firms were not permitted to bid, so their beta is infinity. The social welfare of the home country, before liberalization, is the sum of the expected tax revenue and expected net gains by domestic firms:

$$W^b = \sum_{i \in D} \left(p_i^b R_i - s_i^b \right) \tag{58}$$

In the second scenario, foreign firms are allowed to bid, that is, the β^f fall. There are n^f foreign firms which thus cross the threshold and become active rent-seekers. The social welfare of the home country, after liberalization, is then:

$$W^a = \sum_{i \in D} \left(p_i^a R_i - s_i^a \right) + \sum_{j \in F} p_j^a t R_j \tag{59}$$

The second sum, being the tax revenue from foreign profits, is positive. Thus, there is a net welfare gain, if, and only if, the (before-tax) expected net gain to domestic firms falls by less than the expected tax revenue collected from the foreign firms. We will show that:

$$\sum_{i \in D} \left(p_i^b R_i - s_i^b \right) > \sum_{i \in D} \left(p_i^a R_i - s_i^a \right) \tag{60}$$

Before doing so, we must establish a few preliminary results.

Proposition 7: *The probability of success of any active domestic firm falls after entry of a foreign firm.*

Proof:

$$p_i^b = \frac{g_i^b}{G^b} = 1 - G^b y_i > 1 - G^a y_i = \frac{g_i^a}{G^a} = p_i^a \tag{61}$$

Proposition 8: *The expected profit (whether before or after tax) of each active domestic firm falls after a foreign entry.*

Proof: The change in expected after-tax net profit is:

$$\left(p_i^a - p_i^b \right) \frac{1}{y_i} + \left(g_i^b - g_i^a \right) \tag{62}$$

The first term is negative. The second term is negative if $\gamma_i < \gamma_e$, that is, if firm i is very efficient.

For inefficient firms, $g_i^a < g_1^b$, so the second term is positive. However, we can show that the first term dominates, so that the expected profit falls after entry. In order to see this, note that:

$$\pi_i^a = g_i^a \left[\frac{1}{\gamma_i G^a} - 1 \right] < g_i^b \left[\frac{1}{\gamma_i G^a} - 1 \right] < g_i^b \left[\frac{1}{\gamma_i G^b} - 1 \right] = \pi_i^b \tag{63}$$

Example 4: We continue with example 3 in the preceding section. Suppose $\beta_1 = \beta_2 = 1$, $R_1 = 10$ and $R_2 = 5$.
Before entry,

$$p_1^b = \frac{g_1^b}{g_1^b + g_2^b} = \frac{2}{3} \tag{64}$$

$$\sum_{i=1}^{2} p_i R_i = \frac{25}{3}$$

$$\sum_{i=1}^{2} s_i^b = 3$$

$$W^b = \frac{16}{3} = 5.33$$

Suppose that only one foreign firm enters. After entry,

$$p_1^a = \frac{2.4}{0.8 + 0.8 + 2.4} = 0.6 \tag{65}$$

$$p_2^a = \frac{0.8}{0.8 + 0.8 + 2.4} = 0.2$$

$$s_1^a + s_2^b = 2.4 + 0.8 = 3.2$$

It follows that $W^a > 5.33$ if, and only if, $tR_3 > 7.66$.

Suppose $t=0.5$. Then the net social gain is positive if and only if $R_3 > 15.33$.

Since we have assumed that $y_3 = \dfrac{1}{v_3} = \dfrac{\beta_3^f}{(1-t)R_3} = \dfrac{1}{5}$, the condition that

$R_3 > 15.33$ implies that $\beta_3^f = \dfrac{(1-t)R_3}{5} > 1.533$. Thus, if the domestic firm's lobbying effort is about 50 per cent more effective than that of the foreign counterpart, and the foreign firm's operating net revenue is about 50 per cent more than that of the most efficient domestic firm, there will be a net gain in social welfare when the foreign firm is permitted to lobby for government procurement.

6. Mean-preserving Spreads

Given the set of values $\{y_1, y_2,..., y_m\}$, let $n<m$ be the equilibrium number of active rent-seekers. Then the equilibrium total effective lobbying expenditure is:

$$G^b = \frac{n-1}{Y_m} \tag{66}$$

and the equilibrium effective lobbying expenditure of player i is

$$g_i^b = G^b\left(1 - G^b y_i\right) = \frac{n-1}{Y_n}\left[1 - \frac{(n-1)y_i}{Y_n}\right] \tag{67}$$

Firm $n+1$ will enter as an active player if, and only if, y_{n+1} is lower than the threshold level $Y_n/(n-1)$:

$$y_{n+1} < \frac{Y_n}{n-1} \tag{68}$$

He would not enter if $y_{n+1} \geq Y_n/(n-1)$.

Given n active agents, consider a mean-preserving spread (MPS) in the distribution $\{y_1, y_2,..., y_m\}$. Such an MPS does not encourage entry of the player $n+1$ as long as the new y_n remains lower than y_{n+1}. Now, consider instead a mean-preserving spread (MPS) in the distribution $\{v_1, v_2,..., v_m\}$.

Proposition 9: *A mean-preserving spread of the distribution of the y_i's of the domestic firms will not encourage entry of the foreign firms, but a mean-preserving spread of the distribution of the v_i's of the domestic firms may encourage foreign entries.*

Proof: Suppose, for simplicity, that n is an even integer, and the first $n/2$ active players have effective valuation $v_i = v + \varepsilon$ (where $v > \varepsilon > 0$), and the remaining $n/2$ active players have effective valuation $v_i = v - \varepsilon$. A small increase in ε represents a mean-preserving spread of the distribution $\{v_1, v_2, ..., v_m\}$. Such an MPS increases Y_n, because

$$Y_n = \sum_i \frac{1}{v_i} = (n/2)\frac{1}{v+\varepsilon} + (n/2)\frac{1}{v-\varepsilon} = \frac{n}{2}\left(\frac{2v}{v^2 - \varepsilon^2}\right) \tag{69}$$

and

$$\frac{\partial Y_n}{\partial \varepsilon} > 0 \tag{70}$$

7. Concluding Remarks

We have shown that a relaxation of rules which restrict foreign firms from participating in contests for government procurements can increase domestic welfare. Several factors contribute to this result. First, the aggregate lobbying efforts of all domestic firms may fall. Second, foreign lobbying which uses domestic resources is not a social waste (from the point of view of the host country). Third, the foreign firm may be more profitable, which contributes more to the tax revenue of the host country.

Ngo Van Long, Department of Economics, McGill University, Montréal, Québec, Canada. Email: ngo.long@mcgill.ca

References

Hillman, Arye L. and John Riley. 1989. 'Politically Contestable Rents and Transfers', *Economics and Politics*, 1(1): 17–39. (See also their UCLA Working Paper 452, 1988, bearing the same title.)

Nitzan, S. 1994. 'Modelling Rent-seeking Contests', *European Journal of Political Economy*, 10(1): 41–60.

Rowley, C., R. Tollinson and G. Tullock. 1988. *The Political Economy of Rent-seeking*. Dordrecht and Boston: Kluwer Academic Publishers..

Tullock, G. 1980. 'Efficient Rent-seeking' in J.M. Buchanan, R. Tollinson and G. Tullock (eds), *Toward a Theory of Rent-seeking Society*, College Station: Texas A&M University Press.

The Extent of Exchange Rate Flexibility in India: Basket Pegger or Closet US Dollar Pegger?

Tony Cavoli*
School of Commerce, University of South Australia, Adelaide, Australia

Ramkishen S. Rajan*
School of Public Policy, George Mason University, VA, USA

This article examines the degree of *de facto* exchange rate flexibility for India over the last two decades. While there is a diversity of methods that measure *de facto* exchange rate regimes, none individually encapsulates all the applicable characteristics of an actual regime. It is therefore essential to employ a range of measures so that as many of the salient characteristics possible are captured, as well as to ensure the robustness of the results. While the Reserve Bank of India (RBI) is commonly believed to target the Real Effective Exchange Rate (REER), the results in this article indicate that the Indian rupee is predominantly influenced by the US dollar, with the euro slowly gaining in significance as well.

JEL Classification: F31, F33
Keywords: India, Currency basket, Managed float, Real Effective Exchange Rate (REER), Reserve Bank of India (RBI)

1. Introduction

A defining characteristic of developing Asia as an economic entity is the acute intra-regional heterogeneity that exists among Asian economies, in terms of levels of economic development, rates of economic growth and

*Valuable research assistance by Surabhi Jain and Sadhana Srivastava and comments by participants at the Claremont-Freeman sponsored session at the Singapore Economic Review Conference are gratefully appreciated. The usual disclaimer applies.

economic structures. A similar degree of heterogeneity is apparent in the types of exchange rate regimes officially operated by Asian central banks. For instance, China and Malaysia maintained firm US dollar (USD) pegged regimes until 21 July 2005, and Hong Kong continues to do so. Korea, Philippines, Thailand and Indonesia officially operate inflation targeting regimes with the interest rate as the monetary policy instrument (Cavoli and Rajan 2005). India and Singapore are commonly believed to operate managed floats in the sense of targeting the effective or trade-weighted exchange rate. In particular, while the Monetary Authority of Singapore (MAS) has officially targeted its nominal effective exchange rate (NEER) (around a band) since 1981, it is generally believed that the RBI targets the REER, at least over the medium term (Kumaraswamy 2003).[1]

While recent research has focused on East Asia (see Cavoli and Rajan 2005, on Indonesia, Korea, Philippines and Thailand, and Cavoli and Rajan 2006, on Singapore), scant attention has been paid to India, which is a large and rapidly growing economy and is gradually integrating with the global economy (Figure 1 summarizes trends in India's balance of payments). This article focuses on the degree of *de facto* exchange rate flexibility. How flexible is the Indian rupee (INR), and to the extent that the INR is managed, what is it being managed against, that is, the USD, euro, yen, or a basket of currencies? These are some of the issues explored in this article.

Diverse methods are commonly used to measure *de facto* exchange rate regimes. However, no single measure encapsulates all the applicable characteristics of an actual regime. It is, therefore, essential to employ a range of measures so that maximum number of the salient characteristics of each regime are captured, as well as to ensure the robustness of the results. Section 2 examines the degree of influence that a vector of major currencies has on the home currency. This is done by employing Frankel and Wei (1994) regressions for the INR.[2] The method essentially involves conducting an Ordinary Least Squares (OLS) test of the local currency on other currencies that are considered to influence the former. The basic estimation is augmented here by employing time-varying parameter estimation techniques through recursive OLS. Section 3 constructs and examines two exchange rate flexibility indices centred on the nexus between exchange rates and

---

[1] We say 'generally believed' as the RBI has, since 1993, officially stated that the focus of its exchange rate policy is to 'manage volatility'. Of course this could mean many things. Joshi and Sanyal (2004) argue that India has been pursuing REER targeting with respect to five target currencies, viz., US, Japan, UK, Germany and France at the 1993–94 level.

[2] Such regressions have recently been used in several subsequent studies, including McKinnon (2001), Gan (2000) and Cavoli and Rajan (2005, 2006).

FIGURE 1

Trends in India's balance of payments transactions, 1990–2004

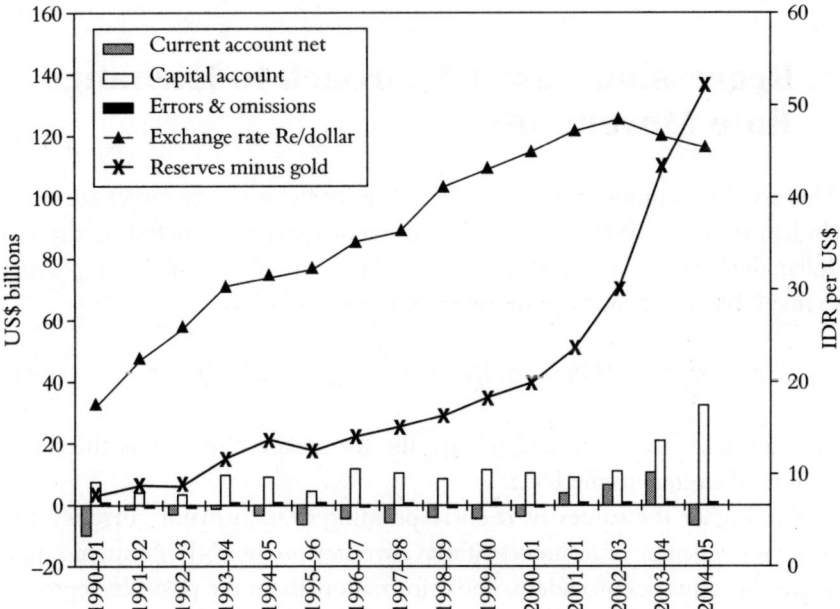

Source: Reserve Bank of India (RBI) and www.indiainfoline.com
Note: India's fiscal year is from 1 April to 31 March.

foreign reserves. The first involves some preliminary testing around a simple index, while the second constructs an alternative index, based on those from Baig (2001), Bayoumi and Eichengreen (1998), and Glick and Wihlborg (1997). Section 4 further examines the degree of exchange rate flexibility by using a simple Generalised Autoregressive Conditional Heteroskedasticity (GARCH) technique such as that found in Dominguez (1998), and Guimãeres and Karacagdag (2004). Section 5 concludes the article with a brief summary.

Note that unless otherwise stated, the empirical analysis in the article is based on monthly observations for the period 1985:1 to 2004:12.[3] The data is from the IMF International Financial Statistics (IFS). Exchange rate data are taken from line RF (RH for the pound sterling) and the cross rates for the local currency against the yen, pound, euro and Swiss franc are calculated from the quoted bilateral exchange rates. Foreign reserves data for India are calculated as net foreign assets (*line 11–line 16c*) scaled by lagged money base

[3] Data using euros are for the period 1999:1 to 2004:12.

(*line 14*). The NEER and REER data for India are from the RBI (www.rbi.org.in).

2. Regression-based Approach to Exchange Rate Movements

This section examines the degree of influence between the target currency (Indian rupee or INR) and a vector of major currencies including the US dollar, the Japanese yen, the UK pound and the euro. We do this by employing Frankel–Wei regressions as shown in Equation 1 below:

$$\Delta e_t = \alpha_0 + \alpha_1 \Delta US_t + \alpha_2 \Delta JP_t + \alpha_3 \Delta UK_t + \alpha_4 \Delta EU_t + \mu_t \qquad (1)$$

All currencies are expressed in logs, the numeraire currency is the Swiss franc, and e refers to the INR.

The higher the values of α corresponding to each major currency, the larger is the degree of influence of that currency on the INR. As such, a high degree of influence provides some information about the possible degree to which the local currency is fixed to the major currency. However, a large (close to 1) coefficient value does not automatically imply a pegged exchange rate; it may merely reflect a naturally occurring market-driven correlation between two currencies. As such, the standard deviation of the α coefficients provides additional useful information. A small standard deviation is more likely to imply an attempt to systematically maintain the correlation between two currencies by way of intervention (Baig 2001), whereas a larger one potentially supports the idea of the two currencies being naturally correlated. We use a time series of monthly observations from 1985:1 to 2004:12 for most of the regressions except in the case of the euro wherein the sample is 1999:1 to 2004:12. This allows us to examine the particular significance of the euro as a major currency since it actually came into existence.

The standard time-invariant OLS estimates for India are summarized in Table 1. It is noticeable that the USD is the dominant currency in determining the value of the INR (about 80 per cent), both in magnitude and in statistical significance (also see Shah and Patnaik 2005). The influences of both the yen and the pound appear to be small and are statistically insignificant. Another noticeable result is the economic and statistical significance of the euro parameter for the estimates in the second and third columns of Table

1, as well as an increase in the overall goodness of fit.[4] This is suggestive of the euro becoming a more significant currency in determining movements in the Indian rupee post-1999 (about 20 per cent). However, it is somewhat unclear whether the euro's t-stat (2.01–2.63) is actually indicative of policy intervention or is capturing market-induced movements. In other words, we are not able to clearly decipher whether the results are capturing the possibility that the RBI is closely pegging the INR to the euro as a conscious policy decision, or merely reflecting a market-driven phenomenon (since Europe is India's largest trading partner). The relative insignificance of the yen on the INR—in contrast to East Asian currencies (see Cavoli and Rajan 2005, 2006)—is understandable in view of the rather weak economic linkages between the two countries with regard to trade also (and investment) (Table 2).

TABLE 1

Frankel–Wei OLS estimates

Dependent variable	Indian rupee	Indian rupee	Indian rupee
Constant	0.01(4.46)***	0.00(0.47)	0.00(0.53)
US dollar	0.83(17.43)***	0.90(19.18)***	0.86(15.65)***
Japanese yen	0.03(0.48)	0.07(1.52)	0.06(1.36)
UK pound	0.07(1.16)	–	0.11(1.22)
Euro	–	0.28(2.43)**	0.25(2.01)**
Adj R-sq	0.62	0.90	0.90
DW	1.76	1.64	1.63
Obs	241	72	72

Source: Authors.

Notes: Figures in brackets are t-stats. All currencies are expressed per Swiss Franc and are in log differences. (*), (**) and (***) represent 10 per cent, 5 per cent and 1per cent significance levels, respectively.

We expand the Frankel–Wei analysis by re-estimating Equation 1, using recursive OLS estimates. Recursive OLS simply involves estimation of the equation by repeatedly using sub-sets of the sample data that are increased by one observation with each iteration.[5] Such recursive estimates allow us to

---

[4] Given the possibility of multi-collinearity between the euro and pound sterling, we consider a specification with the euro and pound included simultaneously, as well as the case without the sterling. As can be seen from Table 1, the results are largely unchanged.

[5] We estimated the initial regression by using the same number of observations as there are coefficients to be estimated in the α vector. Thus, the first 18 months of values are volatile and ignored given the low degrees of freedom. As a robustness exercise, we also employ Kalman Filter tests, of which recursive OLS is a special case. The results are broadly unchanged and, therefore, not reported here.

TABLE 2

Direction of merchandise trade, 2002*

	Export share (%)	Import share (%)	Total trade share (%)**
		India	
USA	20.7	7.2	13.4
Eurozone-12	21.9	20.4	21.1
UK	4.7	4.5	4.6
Japan	3.5	3.0	3.2
Emerging Asia***	12.0	14.6	13.4
Others	37.2	50.2	44.2
Total	100	100	100

Source: Directorate General of Commerce and Industry, India
Notes: *India's fiscal year for 2002–2003.
　　　　**Total trade = Exports plus Imports.
　　　　***Emerging Asia includes ASEAN, Korea and China and India.

track the evolution of the α coefficients over time. It thus allows us to ascertain whether one of the major currencies is becoming more or less influential in comparison to another.

The results of the recursive regressions are presented in Figure 2. Each figure contains the dynamic properties of the coefficients for the USD, the Japanese yen, the pound and the euro. The influence of the euro is especially apparent in the latter part of the sample. Figure 2 makes clear that the USD is clearly the dominant influence on the INR over the sample. It is noticeable that the influence of the USD has actually increased over the sample from about 0.6 to around 0.9. It can also be seen that, from 1985 to 1993, the degree of influence of the pound was around 0.2 to 0.3, but from 1993 onwards, it became all but negligible. Note also that the influence of the yen increased slightly post 1999. After a period of some fluctuation, the influence of the euro on the INR seems to be increasing. Interestingly, while the euro's influence on the INR has risen quite markedly in significance over the last few years, it has not done so at the expense of the USD.[6]

3. Exchange Rate Flexibility Indices

Another common measure of exchange rate behaviour, adopted in this article, is the exchange rate flexibility index. There are a number of different types of such indices based on the idea of exchange market pressure (EMP). The

---

[6] This leaves us with the next question as to exactly what type of USD pegger India is. We return to this issue in Section 5.

FIGURE 2

Recursive OLS estimates of Frankel–Wei regression

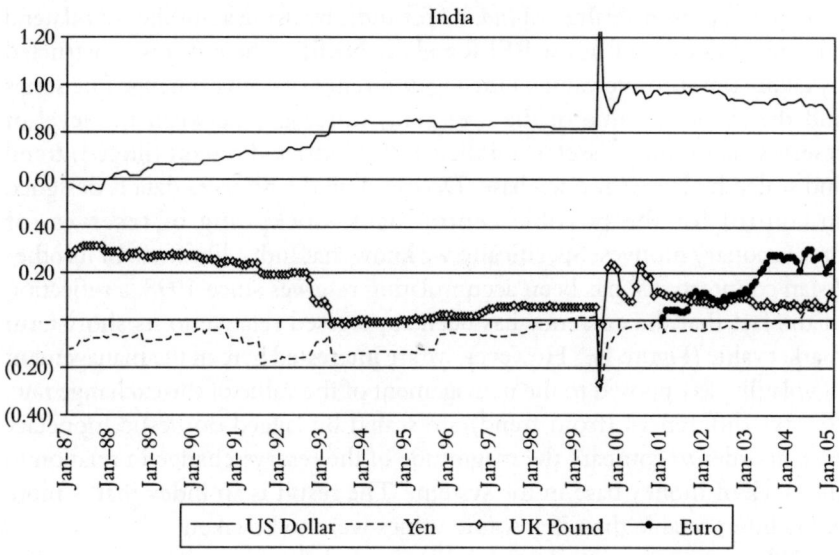

Source: Authors.

theoretical foundation for EMP stems from a basic monetary model incorporating the demand for money, its supply and relative purchasing power parity (PPP) (see for instance, the seminal contribution from Girton and Roper 1977, as also Pentecost, et al. 2001, Guimãeres and Karacadag 2004, and Tanner 2001).

$$Index \ 1 = \Delta e - \Delta f = \Delta d - \Delta p^* - \beta \Delta y + \alpha \Delta i \qquad (2)$$

Equation 2 is the usual equation for EMP. The level of flexibility of an exchange rate regime (or the degree of exchange market pressure) can be ascertained from the left-hand side of equation 2—the relationship between the exchange rate and foreign reserves, $(\Delta e - \Delta f)$.[7] A low index value in this instance may imply either less exchange rate flexibility or a higher level of intervention. Other things being equal, a higher reserve volatility reduces the index value, possibly suggesting that reserves are being employed as a monetary policy tool in order to limit the exchange rate flexibility. A caveat is in order. Ideally, one would need to cleanse the reserve data to focus only on reserves change due to policy intervention rather than valuation changes.

---

[7] The other variables in equation (2) are, respectively, change in domestic credit, change in foreign prices, change in foreign output, and change in the domestic interest rate.

However, this is not possible, as most countries do not provide data on the currency composition of reserves.

Figure 3 presents values of *Index 1* for India by using a number of bilateral currency pairs as well as the REER and the NEER. The index is constructed by taking the absolute value of the log difference of each exchange rate series and the absolute value of the (per cent) difference between the level of reserves (net foreign assets) and their HP (Hodrick–Prescott filtered) trend and scaled by lagged money base. De-trending the reserves data is designed to control for the possible central bank stockpiling of reserves for precautionary motives. Specifically, we know that India, like most of its other Asian counterparts, has been accumulating reserves since 1998, a reflection of the fact that the currency has been suppressed relative to its short-term market value (Figure 1).[8] However, we are interested here in the management of volatility as opposed to the management of the value of the exchange rate. Reserve differences (from trend) are scaled by lagged domestic monetary base in order to compare the magnitude of the reserve change in relation to the stock of money base in the system.[9] The result is an index that is more easily interpretable than if absolute values were to be taken.

Table 3 presents some descriptive statistics and stationarity test results for *Index 1* for India. From the individual currency pairings in Table 3, it can be seen that the mean and median index values for the exchange rate versus the US dollar (USD) are lower than the others. This signifies the possibility of intervention in that currency pair (INR/USD), while the higher mean/ median values for the other currency pairs and the higher standard deviation in the yen provides evidence of additional exchange rate flexibility (or less intervention). Importantly, these figures confirm the Frankel–Wei tests in the previous section wherein a high degree of influence of the USD on the INR was revealed.

We can use *Index 1* to investigate whether the index has changed over time. This might offer evidence of a change in regime or a change in the index value of one currency at the expense of another. As such, we conduct stationarity tests to ascertain if there is any mean-reversion in the data. Table 3 also presents the results of two such tests for each country and currency, such as ADF and Kwiatkowski-Phillips-Schmidt-Shin (KPSS).[10] All the ADF

---

[8]   See Willett et al. (2005) for a discussion of problems with trends in reserves data and various ways of dealing with it.

[9]   This method of measuring reserve changes is quite common in the EMP literature (for instance, see Baig 2001; Bayoumi and Eichengreen 1998; Pentecost et al. 2001; Tanner 2001. We will consider these measures at a later stage.

[10]   It is well-known that the ADF test has low power in predicting the difference between unit root and near-unit root processes. As such, the KPSS test for stationarity is included for robustness. The lag length for ADF and KPSS tests are selected by applying the Schwartz criteria.

FIGURE 3

Index 1, **Exchange rate flexibility index for Indian rupee**

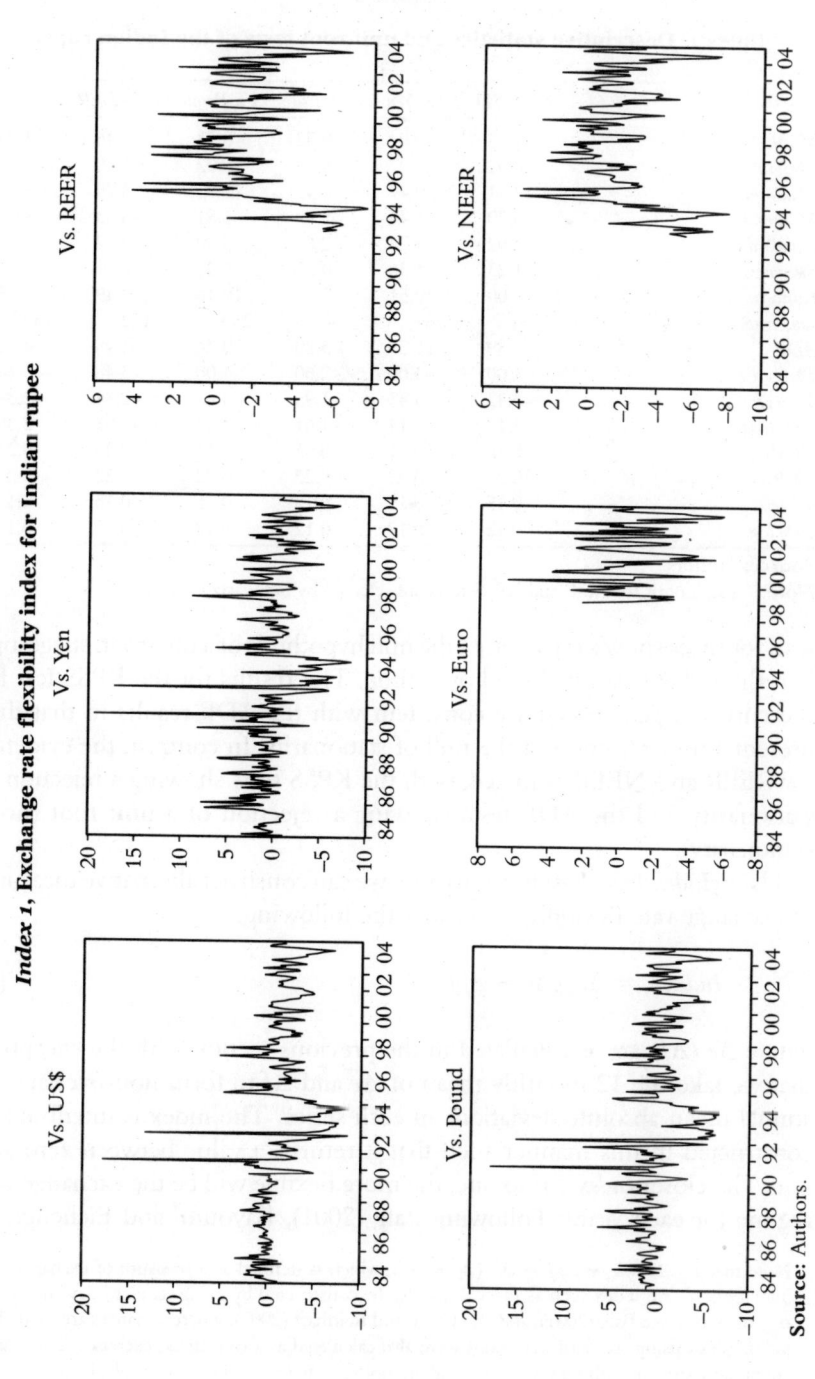

Source: Authors.

TABLE 3

Index _1_, Descriptive statistics and unit root tests of the Indian rupee

	Vs. USD	Vs. Yen	Vs. Euro	Vs. Pound	Vs. REER	Vs. NEER
Mean	−1.33	0.04	−0.72	−0.23	−1.46	−1.84
Median	−0.92	−0.07	−0.68	0.02	−1.30	−1.49
Maximum	17.91	19.47	6.43	17.93	3.79	3.98
Minimum	−8.79	−8.40	−5.98	−6.81	−8.33	−8.09
Standard dev.	2.92	3.24	2.66	3.00	2.32	2.39
Skewness	1.23	1.36	0.27	1.22	−0.41	−0.34
Kurtosis	12.00	10.51	2.89	10.16	3.49	2.95
Observations	250	250	70	250	122	139
ADF	−6.89	−11.28	−5.20	−9.74	−4.98	−4.71
1% level	−4.00	−4.00	−2.60	−4.00	−3.48	−3.48
5% level	−3.43	−3.43	−1.95	−3.43	−2.88	−2.88
10% level	−3.14	−3.14	−1.61	−3.14	−2.58	−2.58
KPSS	0.16	0.11	0.05	0.11	0.25	0.24
1% level	0.22	0.22	0.22	0.22	0.22	0.22
5% level	0.15	0.15	0.15	0.15	0.15	0.15
10% level	0.12	0.12	0.12	0.12	0.12	0.12

Source: Authors.
Note: Lag length for ADF and KPSS tests are selected by Schwartz Criteria.

tests for India show a rejection of the null hypothesis of a unit root, suggesting that the index has not shifted over time. The results for the KPSS test for the currency _pairs_ tested are consistent with the ADF results in that they present a non-rejection of the null of stationarity. In contrast, the evidence for REER and NEER is mixed, with the KPSS tests showing a rejection of stationarity and the ADF tests showing a rejection of a unit root (non-stationarity).

Using _Index 1_ as a baseline measure, we can construct alternative measures of exchange rate flexibility. Consider the following:

$$Index\ 2 = \Delta e\ /(\Delta e + \Delta f) \tag{3}$$

where $\Delta e\ (\Delta f)$ are as calculated in the previous section with the exception that we take the 12 monthly mean of Δe and Δf to form non-overlapping annual mean absolute deviations in each series. The index is intentionally constructed in this manner such that it returns a value between zero and one. The closer _Index 2_ is to one, the more flexible will be the exchange rate regime for each year.[11] Following Baig (2001), Bayoumi and Eichengreen

---

[11] Note that $1 - \Delta e\ /(\Delta e + \Delta f) = \Delta f\ /(\Delta e + \Delta f)$, which is defined as a measure of exchange rate intervention. An index such as _Index 2_ can also be constructed by using standard deviations, e.g. $\sigma_{\Delta e}/\sigma_{\Delta e} + \sigma_{\Delta f}$. See Baig (2001), and also Calvo and Reinhart (2002), where variances are used. The index values using standard deviations were also calculated as a robustness exercise. The results are broadly similar to those for _Index 2_ and are not reported here. They are available on request.

(1998) and many others, we exclude interest rate volatility, partly because it is not always clear whether interest rate variations capture policy changes or general market conditions. In addition, even if we could show that the central bank has pursued an activist interest rate policy, it could either be used in support of exchange rate stability (that is the price target) or in defence of a certain target level of reserves (that is the quantity target).

The results of the estimations of *Index 2* are highlighted in Figure 4. It is apparent that the Indian rupee's flexibility against the yen, pound and euro has remained quite high over the entire sample period. The degree of flexibility of the USD seems to have reduced materially since about 1996. Of particular significance is the fact that after 1996, the index of the INR vis-à-vis the USD has consistently been lower than even the REER-based index, indicating a possible USD peg in the latter part of the sample. The results are consistent with those of *Index 1* and the Frankel–Wei tests with regard to the important role played by the USD in 'impacting' the INR.

FIGURE 4

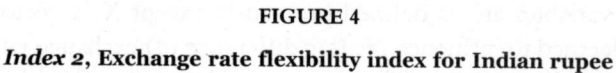

Index 2, Exchange rate flexibility index for Indian rupee

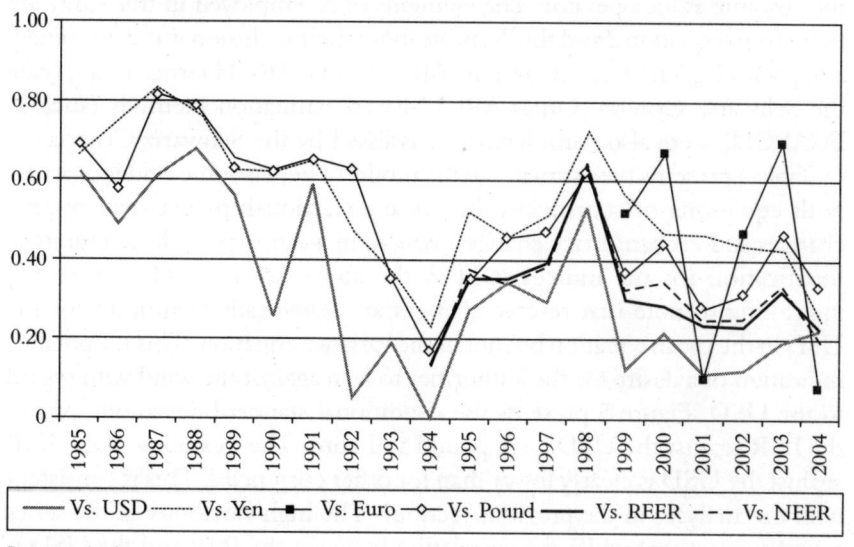

Source: Authors.

4. Simple GARCH Model of Indian Rupee

The final method of examining exchange rate flexibility is to estimate a simple GARCH model. The GARCH model essentially allows us to observe the conditional volatility of the exchange rate, h_t, once the influence of the effect of possible intervention and other influences are controlled for. In effect, it provides information about the underlying flexibility of a currency. We are interested in estimating a simple model with a view to assessing the relationship between reserves and the exchange rate, and to investigate whether the results are consistent with the results in previous sections. As with Dominguez (1998), the effect of possible intervention (using reserves) is captured in the mean equation, equation 3 by Δf_t, and in the variance equation, equation 5, by its absolute value $|\Delta f_t|$.[12] We estimate the following model:

$$\Delta e_t = b_0 + b_1(L)\Delta e_{t-1} + b_2\Delta f_t + b_3 X_t + \mu_t \qquad (4)$$

$$\mu_t \sim N(0, h_t) \qquad (5)$$

$$h_t = \beta_0 + \beta_1(L)\,\mu_t^2 + \beta_2(L)h_{t-1} + \beta_3|\Delta f_t| + \beta_4|X_t| + \varepsilon_t \qquad (6)$$

where all variables are as defined previously except X_t, a vector of other variables deemed to influence the (log difference of) exchange rate and $|\cdot|$ is the absolute value operator. The elements of X_t employed in this study are those from equation 2 and the decision about their inclusion was determined, along with lag length for Δe and the ARCH and GARCH terms, by applying the Schwartz Criteria. Other ARCH-based estimation methods (such as EGARCH) were also considered and assessed by the Schwartz Criteria.

Table 4 presents the estimates to the model. There is some evidence across both equations of statistically significant relationships between reserve changes and exchange rate changes, which, in a sense, provide an empirical justification for the indices used in the above sections. However, it is interesting to note that reserve changes are statistically significant for the USD in the mean equation but not in the variance equation. This is a possible indication of a desire for the authorities to lean against the wind with regard to the USD. Figure 5 presents the conditional standard deviations, $\sqrt{h_t}$, of the INR against the USD, yen, pound and euro. The flexibility of the INR against the USD is clearly lower than for other currencies. This is consistent with the analyses in the previous sections. The high variability of the series might suggest that while the correlation between the INR and the USD is high, it might not be reflective of *systematic* intervention.

---

[12] In a recent paper using this technique, Guimarães and Karacadag (2004) adopt an asymmetric component threshold GARCH (ACT-GARCH) model that tests volatility at different time horizons. This is made possible because of the availability of daily intervention data for Mexico and Turkey.

TABLE 4

GARCH estimates for Indian rupee

Dependent variable	Indian rupee per:			
	US	Yen	UK	Euro
Mean equation				
Constant	0.21***	0.68***	0.53***	0.35
Lagged Δe	0.02	0.23***	0.16***	0.31***
Δf	–0.10 ***	–0.03	0.01	0.05
Variance equation				
Constant	0.01	5.76*	1.42**	1.76 ***
ARCH (1)	4.25***	0.06	0.62	0.15***
GARCH (1)	0.08 *	–0.32	0.58***	0.79 ***
ARCH (2)			–0.37	
GARCH (2)			0.09	
$|\Delta f|$	0.02	3.25 **	–0.17 **	–0.48 ***

Source: Authors.

Notes: The table presents estimates from the GARCH model given by Equations 4–6. Lag length and variables present above were selected on the basis of SBC criteria. The exception is Δf as we wish to assess the relationship between it and Δe.

(*), (**) and (***) represents 10 per cent, 5 per cent and 1 per cent significance levels, respectively.

5. Concluding Remarks

Despite the fact that different types of exchange rate flexibility measures are designed to capture different characteristics of exchange rate behaviour, our empirical analysis appears to indicate that there is a great deal of convergence in the way exchange rate regimes can be viewed over the sample. The time-varying coefficients from the recursive OLS tests for India reveal that the US dollar has become increasingly influential towards the latter part of the sample period. This is suggestive of a greater desire by the RBI to manage the currency vis-à-vis the US dollar (also see Shah and Patnaik 2005). The exchange rate flexibility index reiterates this conclusion; the degree of flexibility of the Indian rupee against the US dollar decreased steadily since 1996–97. The recursive OLS tests and the flexibility index also seem consistent with respect to the Indian rupee's movements against other major currencies.

The conclusion that the Indian rupee is a *de facto* soft US dollar peg is consistent with Reinhart and Rogoff (2004), who have classified India as a *de facto* crawling peg to the US dollar (that is, a peg with a drift).[13] To be more

---

[13] Using slightly different exchange rate flexibility indices than those used in this article, Willett et al. (2005), arrive at a similar conclusion on the Indian rupee and even go on to use it as a benchmark for pegged regimes. Also see Patnaik (2004), who concludes that India has been operating a soft US dollar peg and goes on to detail India's experience with managing such an arrangement, focusing on capital flows and reserve build-up.

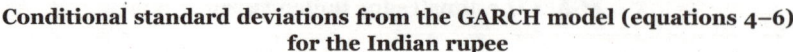

FIGURE 5

Conditional standard deviations from the GARCH model (equations 4–6) for the Indian rupee

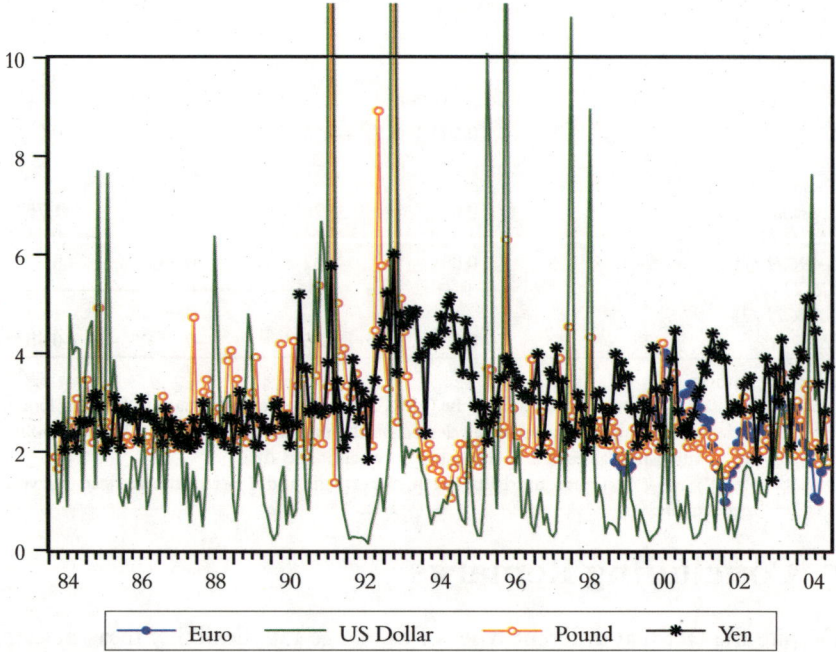

Source: Authors.

specific, Reinhart and Rogoff (2004) characterize India as a *de facto* crawling US dollar peg between July 1995 and December 2001, and a *de facto* peg (no crawl) between August 1991 and June 1995.[14] The empirics in this article also suggest that the euro is gradually gaining greater importance in influencing movements in the Indian rupee, but more so at the expense of the pound and yen rather than the US dollar. If the euro continues to gain in importance, one might have to eventually re-classify India as a (dual) basket peg over time. However, as of now, it seems to be a soft or *de facto* dollar pegger. While India has been relatively successful in its monetary policy framework to date (Joshi and Sanyal 2004), as the country continues to

[14] Reinhart and Rogoff (2004) define a *de facto* peg on the basis of whether a monthly exchange rate change remains within a one per cent band over a rolling five-year period with at least an 80 per cent probability. If the exchange rate has a drift, it is classified as a crawling peg.

liberalize its capital account, continued heavy management of the exchange rate will invariably complicate its overall macroeconomic policies.

Tony Cavoli, School of Commerce, University of South Australia, Adelaide, Australia. Email: tony.cavoli@unisa.edu.au
Ramkishen S. Rajan, School of Public Policy, George Mason University, VA, USA. Email: rrajan1@gmu.edu

References

Baig, T. 2001. 'Characterising Exchange Rate Regimes Post-Crisis East Asia', Working Paper No.01/152, IMF.

Bayoumi, T. and B. Eichengreen. 1998. 'Exchange Rate Volatility Intervention: Implications of the Theory of Optimum Currency', *Journal of International Economics*, 45(2):191–209.

Calvo, G. and C. Reinhart. 2002. 'Fear of Floating', *Quarterly Journal of Economics*, 117(2): 379–408.

Cavoli, T. and R. Rajan. 2005. 'Have Exchange Rate Regimes in Asia Become More Flexible after the Crisis? Revisiting the Evidence', mimeo, April.

———. 2006. 'Managing in the Middle: Characterising Singapore's Exchange Rate Policy', mimeo, February.

Dominguez, K.M. 1998. 'Central Bank Intervention and Exchange Rate Volatility', *Journal of International Money and Finance*, 17(1):161–90.

Frankel, J. and S.J. Wei. 1994. 'Yen Bloc or Dollar Bloc? Exchange Rates in the East Asian Economies' in T. Ito and A. Krueger (eds), *Macroeconomic Linkage: Savings, Exchange Rates, and Capital Flows.* Chicago: University of Chicago Press.

Gan, W.B. 2000. 'Exchange Rate Policy in East Asia after the Fall: How Much Have Things Changed?', *Journal of Asian Economics,* 11(4): 403–30.

Girton, L. and D. Roper. 1977. 'A Monetary Model of Exchange Market Pressure Applied to the Post-War Canadian Experience', *American Economic Review*, 67(4): 537–48.

Glick, R. and C. Wihlborg. 1997. 'Exchange Rate Regimes and International Trade' in P. Kenen and B. Cohen (eds), *International Trade and Finance: New Frontiers for Research*. New York: Cambridge University Press.

Guimāeres, R.F. and C. Karacagdag. 2004. 'The Empirics of Foreign Exchange Intervention in Emerging Market Countries: The Cases of Mexico and Turkey', Working Paper 04/123, IMF.

Joshi, V. and S. Sanyal. 2004. 'Foreign Inflows and Macroeconomic Policy in India', mimeo, Oxford University.

Kumaraswamy, V. 2003. 'Exchange Rates—REER Logic May Be Unsustainable', *Business Line*, February 21.

McKinnon, R. 2001. 'After the Crisis, the East Asian Dollar Standard Resurrected: An Interpretation of High-Frequency Exchange-Rate Pegging' in J. Stiglitz and S. Yusuf (eds), *Rethinking the East Asian Miracle*. New York: World Bank and Oxford University Press.

Patnaik, I. 2004. 'India's Experience with the Implementation of a Pegged Exchange Rate', mimeo, April.

Pentecost, E.J., C. Van Hooydonk and A. Van Poeck. 2001. 'Measuring and Estimating Exchange Market Pressure in the EU', *Journal of International Money and Finance*, 20(3): 401–18.

Reinhart, C.M. and K. Rogoff. 2004. 'The Modern History of Exchange Rate Reinterpretation', *Quarterly Journal of Economics*, 199(1): 1–48.

Shah, A. and I. Patnaik. 2005. 'India's Experience with Capital Flows: The Elusive Quest for a Sustainable Current Account Deficit', Working Paper No.11387, NBER.

Tanner, E. 2001. 'Exchange Market Pressure and Monetary Policy: Asia and Latin America in the 1990s', *IMF Staff Papers*, 47(3):311–33.

Willett, T.D., J. Kim and I. Nitithanprapas. 2005. 'Some Methodological Issues in the Classification of Exchange Rate Regimes', mimeo, July.

The Role of Foreign Firms in India over the Past Half Century: Retrospect and Prospect

SUMIT K. MAJUMDAR
School of Management, University of Texas at Dallas, Richardson

This article evaluates whether the changing presence of foreign firms in India's corporate sector has had an impact on the long-run economic performance of India's industrial sector. The patterns of corporate demography, including the role of foreign firms in India over the last five decades, from the 1950s to the 2000s, are traced and then related to a measure of economic performance calculated in the form of productive efficiency indices for the entire Indian industry for the period from 1957–58 to 2001–02. The results show a strong relationship between the growing presence of foreign firms in India and the productive efficiency of Indian industry. The notion that foreign firms' capabilities can spill over to other sectors of industry finds support, and an increase in the presence of foreign firms is also associated with an enhancement of the Indian industry's ability to utilize its managerial human capital effectively. In the period after reforms, that commenced in 1991, the number of foreign firms operating in India has increased substantially. Thus, foreign firms are interested in increasing their presence in the Indian economy, with positive performance consequences expected from such increased participation. So far, basic property rights changes have had significant effects on providing incentives for foreign firms to operate in India, and the automatic availability of such property rights has been a major factor affecting the motivation of foreign firms to set up operations in India. Yet, the government gave veto rights to the Indian private sector on certain aspects of the entry of foreign firms into India by promulgating Press Note 18 in late 1998, which was repealed in early 2005, and it is difficult to speculate on either the precise number of foreign companies that were scared off by this note or the loss of performance accompanying the absence of foreign firms from Indian industry.

JEL Classification: F23
Keywords: Corporate demography, Economic reforms, Foreign direct investment, Indian industry, Productive efficiency, Property rights, Spillovers

1. Introduction

1.1 The Background

The Indian attitude to foreign investment has been ambiguous. Perhaps as a hangover of the colonial past, during which substantial national wealth and economic resources were indeed lost to the West, there has been wariness as to what types of foreign firms can operate in India. Coupled with Indian intelligentsia's rapid absorption of anti-multinational company (MNC) views, fuelled no doubt in part by examples such as ITT in Allende's Chile and later Enron, there still remains a strong groundswell against the presence of foreign firms in India.

Irrespective of whether this implicit Indian psyche makes its way via osmosis into the minds of negotiators or not, in the present day and age, India has barely managed a few billion dollars a year as foreign direct investment (FDI) inflows. The sums hovered around the $1 billion mark for several years, and highly positive sentiments expressed that in 2004 the sums were around the $3.7 billion mark, though the economy can easily absorb 10 times that amount. For a country with one-fifth of the world's people, one that ranks high on FDI outlook indices, and one that is supposed to be one of the great global powers in the foreseeable future, the annual sum received is trivial; in fact, it is less than 1 per cent, given that global annual FDI flows are worth hundreds of billions of dollars, and China alone receives over $50 billion per year. In addition, FDI in India accounts for less than 5 per cent of all investments made in India. Therefore, the role of FDI in the Indian economy, in an absolute sense, is very small.

Nevertheless, India has had a long history of foreign investment. After 1900, and particularly between 1919 and 1947, there had been a considerable increase in Indian entrepreneurship (Bagchi 1972). At the time of Independence, the predominant share of capital in industry was foreign-owned (Kidron 1965), and India was host to a large body of foreign capital, principally British. As a characteristic of colonial heritage, foreign investments were concentrated in extractive industries; for example, 85 per cent of the area planted with tea was foreign-owned. Another area of concentration was that of international trade and ancillary services. Foreign units also constituted the largest and most influential section in any industry that they participated in. Kidron (1965) documents that the average foreign-owned cotton mill employed 3,300 workers, as compared to 1,800 by an Indian-owned mill. Also, as late as 1951–52, 39 per cent of India's imports, and 37–44 per cent of India's exports were handled by foreign firms.

From the 1950s onwards, however, the policy thrust was on detailed centralized planning, and the role of the state as the premier catalyst of industrial development was codified in industrial policy statements and resolutions (Jalan 1991). While Indian industrial development progressed via the organizational mechanisms of both public and private sector enterprises, the role of foreign capital diminished and there were significant capital reparations. After 1947, the sales of British interests to Indian entrepreneurs continued. While in 1938, there were as many as 61 large business groups controlled by the British, by 1962, no more than 25 business groups remained British (Kidron 1965).

A particular phenomenon, observable after the mid-1950s, was the growth in government-owned enterprises. In 1948, an Industrial Policy Resolution was passed by which the government sought control of industrialization, and this was to be achieved through the Industries (Development and Regulation) Act of 1951. The role of the state as an industrial entrepreneur and manager was clearly articulated, and this articulation of ideas was consistent with the industrial development model being adopted in the Western European countries at that time. However, if private firms existed in certain industries where the state was to assume a dominant role, these firms had the freedom to undertake efficient production and expansion.

In 1956, a second Industrial Policy Resolution was enunciated. This resolution then guided industrial policy-making in India for well over a quarter of a century. The principle that the state was to be the dominant industrializing authority was maintained and the resolution precisely operationalized the nature of public ownership. While private firms were occasionally likely to be authorized to produce items that had earlier been reserved for the state sector, the latter could enter at will into sectors where private firms were dominant players. The second Industrial Policy Resolution coincided with the launch of the Second Five Year Plan in India, an event, which, while decisively channelling resources into the industrial sector also explicitly put into place a mindset signifying that the evolution of the economy was to be guided by conscious human action and choices that were to be made at the New Delhi Secretariat. It was the time when the *commanding heights* argument was clearly articulated.

Two important factors that have shaped the corporate landscape of India during the last half-century have been the relative decline of foreign firms and the growth of government firms. In a sense, the implicit mindset has been one of autarky. The closing of the economy to external capital and the substitution of private domestic capital by government capital were the instruments used in the process. The decline in the role of foreign firms in

India was further exacerbated by the introduction of the Foreign Exchange Regulation Act (FERA) in 1973. While FERA was promulgated after the hike in oil prices in order to save foreign exchange that was needed to pay for critical imports such as food and petroleum, at the same time, the maximum shareholding that foreign firms could have in Indian companies was limited to 40 per cent. This condition was laid down to ensure that outflows repatriated to foreign owners could be minimized. Nevertheless, the consequences were dysfunctional. Das (2002:199) recounts his story of an American businessman remarking, at a meeting with the then Indian Prime Minister, Mrs Indira Gandhi: 'My issue, Madam Prime Minister, is with the government's insistence on limiting foreign ownership in companies to 40 per cent. Consequently, multinational companies have lost interest in India. And your country is neither getting investment nor technology.'

The change of government in 1977 brought together a coalition of political partners which had ambiguous attitudes towards foreign firms. Firms such as IBM and Coca Cola were given marching orders out of India, while firms such as Siemens and Bechtel were welcomed with open arms. The rules limiting foreign ownership to only 40 per cent continued for almost two decades and were finally eliminated after the introduction of economic reforms in 1991, and there has, since then, been a resurgence of entrepreneurial activity in India. Since the advent of reforms, not only has domestic entrepreneurship expanded substantially, but foreign firms have also started making investments in India once again. Simultaneously, a policy of privatization has been adopted which, though not being implemented in a comprehensive manner, recognizes the need for a transformation in the performance of firms that are in public ownership. A substantial evolution in the progress of Indian industry has been taking place since the 1991 reforms, and this progress builds on the pattern of evolution put into place in the mid-1950s.

1.2 The Core Issue Evaluated in this Article

A substantial body of literature (for instance, Buckley and Casson 1976; Dunning 1993; Helpman 1984; Hymer 1976) has highlighted the contours of theoretical concerns showing that foreign firms' performance is superior as compared to that of other firms within an economy. A key view is that foreign firms have superior capabilities, which lead them to become international players in the first place (Caves 1996). They possess several assets including international marketing capabilities, location advantages in other countries, a global operations network, and in-depth knowledge of foreign markets (de la Torre 1974). They also have the ability to manage the international political economy dimension (Helleiner 1988). These ideas find their support in the dynamic capabilities view of the firm that is extant in management literature, and in the contemporary endogenous growth theory.

In fact, Caves (1996) explicitly articulates the view that the firms' motives for overseas forays and successes are significantly predicated upon the possession of intangible assets. Successful firms making overseas investments possess substantial intangible assets. The ownership of these assets serves to enhance the competencies and capabilities that firms possess, and the availability of a stock of capabilities helps the firms leverage these in environmental contexts other than those of the parent country. A major form of an intangible asset is marketing skills. A firm can possess skills in activities such as branding, distribution, merchandizing and promotion such that its product is clearly distinguishable and delivered to the apposite market segment. Another marketing advantage arises from the fact that a foreign firm may operate in several different markets around the world. Such assets are productive as they generate a price premium for the product in question since buyers are willing to pay more for it than for other comparable products or services.

Intangible assets include the availability of superior technologies. These can take the form of patented designs or processes, or manufacturing or research know-how shared among a critical mass of employees. The experiences of the human capital pool that a firm has access to gives it the ability to exploit market opportunities by using superior technologies, at least for the time being. These assets, when deployed in a domestic firm in an emerging market economy with relatively low wage levels, but an educated workforce, also help give decided manufacturing and production cost advantages to foreign firms. This attribute makes their products competitive and leads to relatively superior performance as compared to other firms that operate in the same environment. The pertinent questions that arise in this context are: Would not India have been better off by promoting and increasing the presence of foreign enterprises within its industrial sector? Would not the relative performance of Indian industry have been possibly better because of the presence of foreign firms in India?

1.3 Contours of the Present Study

Using a database created and put together from the records of the Department of Company Affairs (DCA) of the Government of India, this article first traces the patterns of corporate demography in India over the last five decades, from the 1950s to the 2000s, and then, using time series regression techniques, evaluates whether the changing presence of foreign firms in India's corporate sector has had an impact on the long-run economic performance of India's industrial sector. Corporate demography, as a field, deals with the big picture issue of the evolution of the populations of firms and industries, and their impact on various parameters of economic performance such as productivity or employment (Carroll and Hannan 2000). The article is cast within that framework to evaluate the role of foreign firms in India.

The DCA database is a compellingly unique and comprehensive population level coverage of the numbers of various types of companies that make up India's corporate sector. The data are available for several decades in a time series. There is also another comprehensive database, one put together by the Central Statistical Organization (CSO) as the Annual Survey of Industries (ASI). Using these data, and an operational research technique called data envelopment analysis (Charnes et al. 1994), I measure economic performance as productive efficiency of Indian industry, using to do so. The DCA and ASI data both cover the period ranging from 1957–58 to 2001–02, and permit an evaluation of industrial performance over five decades. These also permit an economy-wide analysis. Interpretations of the roles that various types of companies or firms (the term 'firm' is interchangeably used here with companies) have played in the past half a century within the Indian economy are possible.

Capital, be it technological, organizational, human or intellectual, has been expressed as the source of productivity and that of the wealth of nations (de Soto 2000). Such reasoning has to be taken a step further. Productive efficiency, in a dynamic perspective, is the most significant measure of economic performance, since a continuing high level of productivity eventually provides the financial outcomes of undertaking any economic activity and the wherewithal that facilitates further capital investments. It signifies the implicitly unobservable, but explicitly measurable, link between the primary investment of capital, on the one hand, and the generation of further capital surpluses, on the other.

The issue explored in this article is whether the presence of foreign firms in the Indian economy has been positively associated with the productivity of industry as a whole over the past five decades. This is also a standard question in the literature on spillovers, dealing with the efficacy of the presence of different forms of investments within the context of an economy, for which there is a substantial amount of recent evidence (see Balasubramanyam, et al. 1996; Blomstrom and Kokko 1998; Gorg and Strobl 2001). Nevertheless, this evidence is at best ambiguous and equivocal for several countries of the world. For India, an evaluation of the pharmaceutical sector has revealed positive spillovers, but not for the industry in question as a whole (Feinberg and Majumdar 2001). If the long-run presence of foreign firms in the Indian economy has been positively associated with productive efficiency, then the attitudes towards FDI may well deserve a rethinking.

1.4. Empirical Analysis

As remarked above, two sources of data are used for the analyses in this article. A set of evidence showing the growth of the corporate sector, in both absolute and relative terms, is generated by using data that are obtained from the DCA, a department that is specifically interested in the corporate sector of India as a whole. Their data is available at the company or corporate level. They do not, however, look after the interests of businesses that are organized either as proprietorships, partnerships or cooperatives. Nevertheless, firms organized as corporations account for almost 90 per cent of the value of industrial output in India. The second set of data used are generated by the ASI, which is an activity carried out by the CSO.

The DCA data are organized as a time series for the period 1957–58 to 2001–02, and contain details on the number of: (*i*) foreign companies in India; (*ii*) domestic private companies in India; (*iii*) government companies in India; and (*iv*) total companies in India. Details are also provided about companies belonging to the not- for-profit sector, which are very limited in number, and these form the base case left out for subsequent regression analysis in order to ensure that the matrix is not singular. The data covers the entire population of enterprises making up the corporate sector in India. These data provide a full picture of the evolution of India's corporate economy for almost five decades, which have been the critical post-War and for India post-Independence decades when the basic structure of India's economy and society were being developed.

From these data, it is possible to calculate the following ratios that become relevant for carrying out further analyses: (*i*) the proportion of foreign companies, as defined under Section 591 of the Companies Act 1956, to the total number of companies in the corporate sector as a whole; (*ii*) the proportion of domestic private companies to the total number of companies in the corporate sector as a whole; and (*iii*) the proportion of government companies to the total number of companies in the corporate sector as a whole. These statistics provide the overall picture on the evolution of the industrial structure of India for over a 45-year period. However, the total number of observations used, within a time series framework, is 44, since the ASI data were not released for the year 1972–73. Since extensive time series data are available, it is possible to calculate the period-to-period changes for each of the variables so that the impact of the changing presence of a variety of firms can be evaluated.

The article unfolds as follows. Section 2 provides details of the corporate demography of India and discusses the trends that have been noted. Section 3 discusses the analyses of productive efficiency that are carried out and the results that are obtained. The procedure also generates measures of the latent competencies that are prevalent within the Indian industrial sector. This section also highlights the relationships between the different types of firms analyzed and the different latent competencies within Indian industry. Section 4 discusses the implications of the findings and the contours of the changing policy mindset in India. It also highlights some policy changes that are required in order to keep attracting foreign investment. Section 5 sums up the article.

2. The Corporate Demography of India

2.1 The Basic Facts

The approach taken in this article is to highlight the demography of India's corporate sector in a relatively straightforward way, by first describing the different patterns of growth displayed by three types of firms that are important within the context being evaluated: foreign firms, private domestic firms and government firms. In a sense, this part of the article is a counting exercise, as in most corporate demography work, wherein the data and the trends are used to describe and discuss the relative composition of India's corporate sector over a 50-year period. Table 1 provides details of the basic statistics.

Table 1 shows the average number of foreign, domestic, private and government firms within India's corporate sector for the overall period from 1957–58 to 2001–02. The average numbers in the total, for each category, may not provide as much insight as the proportions that each category bears to the whole. The proportion of foreign firms in India is less than 1 per cent of India's firms but their share has ranged from a high figure, accounting for 2.127 per cent of all firms in India to a low one accounting for only 0.165 per cent of all firms in India. Clearly, there has been a substantial rise and fall in the proportion of foreign firms within India's corporate economy. The lowest number of foreign firms was 300 while the maximum number is 1,141.

TABLE 1

Descriptive statistics for the various ownership categories

	Number of foreign firms	Number of private firms	Number of government firms
Average	545	144,139	712
Standard deviation	184	164,518	437
Coefficient of variation	0.337	1.141	0.614
Minimum	300	24,821	74
Maximum	1,141	567,834	1,266

	Percentage of foreign firms to total	Percentage of private firms to total	Percentage of government firms to total
Average	0.975	95.725	0.746
Standard deviation	0.792	2.294	0.400
Coefficient of variation	0.810	0.020	0.540
Minimum	0.165	93.025	0.220
Maximum	2.127	98.991	1.484

Source: Author's computations based on DCA data.

A review of the latter half of Table 1 clearly shows that the domestic private enterprise is the dominant type of enterprise in the Indian industrial landscape, at least in numbers. During the said period as a whole, such enterprises have accounted for 95 per cent of India's companies, but again the minimum and maximum values have ranged from 93 per cent to over 98 per cent, respectively. The upper half of Table 1 shows that at one point, the lowest number of domestic private firms in India was 24,821, but the maximum number of domestic private Indian firms has grown to 567,834. Very clearly, there has been substantial growth in the number of domestic private enterprises in India. This growth is evaluated statistically in a subsequent section.

In line with the growth of domestic private firms in India has been the growth of government-owned firms. While accounting for less than 1 per cent of India's corporate sector for the entire period assessed, with a low of 0.22 per cent and a high of just under 1.5 per cent of India's firms, the number of government firms has grown from 74 to 1,266 during the five decades studied. While this impressive growth in the number of companies is not as robust as that of the growth of the number of domestic private firms in India, it is considerably greater than that of the growth in the number of foreign firms. Also, government-owned firms, at one stage, accounted for the bulk of the capital invested in industry (Majumdar 1998).

Data on the amount of capital invested by foreign companies are not available but evidence has been generated showing that foreign companies account for between a quarter and third of the total sales in India's manufacturing sector (Athreye and Kapur 2001). On the whole, foreign firms have accounted for a relatively larger proportion of India's corporate landscape in numbers relative to government companies, but the growth in numbers of government companies in India has been more pronounced. This finding is in keeping with the pro-public sector and anti-foreign firm attitude that has characterized Indian policy-making for a substantial portion of the five decades.

2.2 Trends in the Growth of the Different Types of Firms

While the above discussion has dealt with the big picture, a more interesting line of analysis revolves around an assessment of the trends on a year-by-year basis. These trends can be easily assessed by using figures, and Figure 1 shows the actual number of foreign and government companies in existence and in operation in India for all the years studied. Figure 1 compares the annual trends in the numbers of both foreign and government companies. These companies do not numerically form a substantial part of the Indian

FIGURE 1

The number of government and foreign companies in India

corporate economy, but are large in terms of capital investments and sales generated.

Figure 1 shows that there were, on an average, 568 foreign companies operating in India from 1957–58 to 1972–73, the year before FERA was promulgated. Policies towards foreign firms were not illiberal. After that year, with the introduction of the draconian 40 per cent foreign ownership limit, the number of foreign companies operating in India went down steadily till the early 1980s. During the period 1977–79, there had been substantial confusion over the role of foreign companies' operations in India. Refusing to dilute their ownership holdings from 100 to 40 per cent, Coca Cola and IBM left India. Taking this as a signal, more companies left India thereafter, and the net position was that by 1981, the number of foreign companies operating in India had fallen to 300.

In 1980, Indira Gandhi returned to power, chastened, and initiated a programme of reforms. While it was not mentioned anywhere that reforms were to be launched, several dysfunctional policies were rectified. For example, the ratification of surplus capacity as part of actual capacity commenced. No radical departures from the existing policy mindsets, were forthcoming, but the need to use the existing capacity in place was well-recognized and 1982 was declared a Productivity Year. Also, product development was thought to be a significant area for industries. For showcasing their abilities to introduce new products at competitive costs, industries would need to prove their mettle. However, this necessitated the articulation of policies encouraging the adoption of new foreign technologies and the establishment of plants with globally competitive scale parameters, as opposed to the fragmentation of capacity among numerous firms.

The fact that empirical reality was being recognized, and the evidence that a change of heart was indeed taking place, are reflected in a statement in the Seventh–Plan document: that the approach of government bodies lay 'not in the extensive powers to control and regulate, but in their efforts to provide technical and administrative guidance to industries. The performance of these tasks will be informed less by legal or procedural codes but by better access to data and knowledge' (Government of India 1985: Section 7.42).

What is visible from Figure 1 is that after the early 1980s, the number of foreign companies operating in India has started rising again. The growth becomes most pronounced after 1991, when full freedom of entry and exit was given to companies, and ownership restrictions, other than in a few select industries such as real estate, media and telecommunications, among others, were removed. The number of foreign companies has increased substantially from the mid-1990s onwards, and by 2001–02, there were over 1,100 foreign companies in operation in India. Large jumps in the number of foreign firms started taking place particularly after FERA was transformed into the Foreign Exchange Management Act (FEMA) in 1999. The change from FERA to FEMA was a significantly symbolic act that has sent a signal about the Indian government's intentions.

Figure 1 shows that the number of government companies have steadily increased, from a low number of 74 in 1957–58 to 1,266 in 2001–02. The maximum upsurge in their number took place between the late 1960s and the late 1970s. This is the period when the socialist approach to economic management was given full rein. The number of government companies overtook the number of foreign companies in India in 1975–76, and this phenomenon is totally consistent with the political economy of India. By 1990, the gap between the numbers of foreign and government companies was the largest. The growth in the number of government companies has, however, started tapering off in the twenty-first century, and there is every indication that, given the rate of growth in numbers, foreign companies may outstrip the number of government companies in India within the current decade.

Figure 2 shows the number of domestic private companies operating in India. It is shown separately from the figure for foreign and government companies so as to handle scale issues within and between the two figures.

FIGURE 2

The number of domestic private companies in India

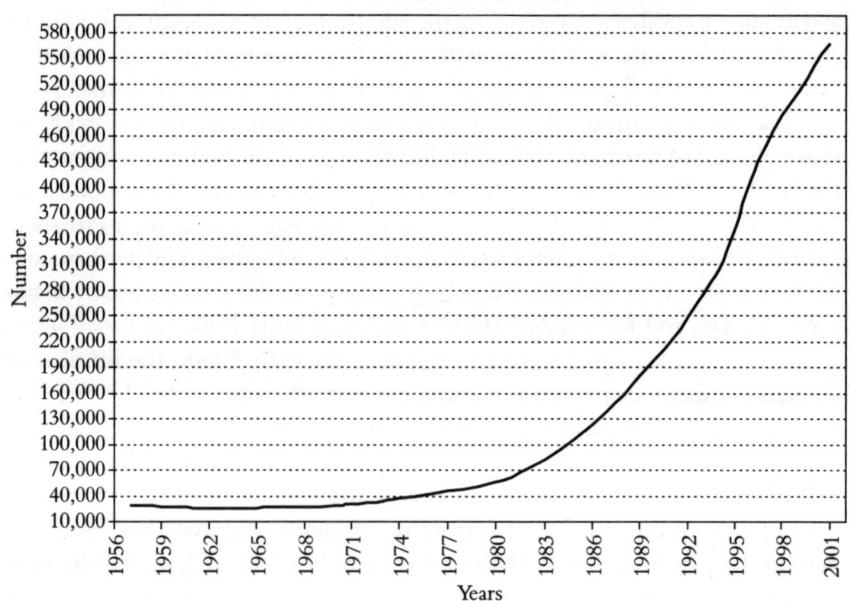

From the 1950s till the late 1970s, there were less than 50,000 domestic private companies operating in India. The curve is quite horizontal during this phase. As remarked earlier, in the early 1980s, there was a change of heart, subtle and unannounced though it might have been, reflecting a desire to encourage private industry. From the 1980s onwards, the number of domestic private companies operating in India has increased very substantially. The curve inclines more towards the vertical from the early 1990s onwards, reflecting the profound sense of entrepreneurship that became apparent in India after the liberalization of 1991. By 2001–02, there were over 550,000 domestic companies operating in India. Nevertheless, domestic private companies in India are of considerably smaller in size than the foreign and government companies that operate in India. India's industrial economy can be characterized as being large-scale in the foreign and government sectors while it is of small- and medium-scale in the domestic sector. This issue of scale is not explicitly addressed in this article but is a topic that ought to be addressed in future analysis.

2.3 Assessing Growth Rates of the Different Types of Firms

Two additional analyses are carried out and reported. Table 2 provides the growth rates for two variables. These are, first, the change in the number of the different types of companies, and second, the change in the proportion that each type of company bears to the total number of companies. The first is an absolute measure. The second is a relative measure that captures the importance of each type of company within the overall number of companies, though in this article it is not possible to evaluate the relative importance in terms of the sales or output generated or in terms of capital invested. Such an analysis is left for future work since it does necessitate the acquisition of more detailed data. Table 3 contains a correlation matrix between the numbers of foreign, private domestic and government companies, and the proportions of foreign, private and government companies.

Panel A of Table 2 displays the annual percentage growth rates, and while foreign firms have grown by an average of just under 2 per cent in number, the numbers of domestic and government firms in India have grown at over 7 per cent, on average, in the entire period. There has been substantial variation in the growth of the number of foreign firms, as also shown in Figure 1, while the numerical growth of private domestic and government companies, or firms, has been steady and has shown limited comparative variation. This is prima facie an indication of an ambivalent, and perhaps even hostile, attitude that has been displayed towards foreign firms operating in India.

TABLE 2

Growth rates for firms belonging to the different ownership categories

	Panel A: Change in the number of firms		
	Foreign firms	*Private firms*	*Government firms*
Average	1.948	7.300	7.042
Standard deviation	6.866	5.943	7.052
Minimum	−24.313	−4.490	−0.333
Maximum	13.697	15.960	27.333
	Panel B: Change in the composition of firms		
	Percentage of foreign firms to total	*Percentage of private firms to total*	*Percentage of government firms to total*
Average	−4.670	0.129	0.356
Standard deviation	7.133	0.172	10.537
Minimum	−28.792	−0.309	−13.692
Maximum	5.439	0.445	27.351

Source: Author's computations.

TABLE 3

Correlations between growth rates of numbers and proportions of various types of firms

	Number of foreign firms	*Number of private firms*	*Number of government firms*	*Proportion of foreign firms*	*Proportion of private firms*
Number of private firms	0.256				
Number of government firms	−0.405	−0.441			
Proportion of foreign firms	0.693	−0.516	−0.016		
Proportion of private firm	−0.258	0.729	−0.114	−0.768	
Proportion of government firms	−0.390	−0.816	0.876	0.271	−0.467

Source: Author's computations.

Panel B of Table 2 displays the annual percentage growth rates in the proportions that each type of company bears to the total number of companies operating within India. This is an important statistic as it shows the relative rise or decline in importance of each type of company. Again, within the period of five decades as a whole, the role of foreign firms has diminished substantially within India and there is a decline, or negative growth, of over 4.6 per cent on an average in the proportion of foreign firms to the total number of firms in India. The proportion of private domestic firms to the total number of firms has not changed materially; on an average, it rises at the rate of 0.13 per cent per annum and this category of company, while growing steadily, has retained its relative position in numbers within the total population of Indian firms. Correspondingly, the proportion of government firms to the total number of firms has changed more substantially, rising, on an average, at 0.36 per cent per annum, during the entire period. These statistics are not at all surprising, given the anti-foreign and pro-government firm attitude that was prevalent for much of the period evaluated.

Here let us dwell briefly on two interesting patterns shown in the correlation matrix in Table 3. First, the growth in the number of government firms in India is negatively correlated with the number of foreign (–0.405) firms and private domestic firms (–0.441) in India. This is an indication that the growth in numbers of government firms has crowded out both private domestic and foreign firms from Indian industry, and, while this is not at all a surprising finding, given the political economy behind India's industrial policy, the correlations coefficients are not insubstantial. Second, the growth in the proportion of foreign firms is negatively correlated with the growth of domestic private firms (0.768). While private domestic firms can also crowd out other forms of firms and other types of capital from industry, this statistic indicates more of a resurgence in private domestic industrial activity signifying that the relative role of private domestic firms is increasing, and eventually private domestic capital is becoming the dominant feature in Indian industry.

The year-by-year detailed numbers that make up the summary statistics as presented in Table 2 and discussed in Sub-section 3.3 are graphically displayed in Figures 3 and 4. Additionally, statistical tests are run on these numbers to evaluate whether the trends are significant or not. First, the trends as shown in Figures 3 and 4 are briefly discussed.

The figures show the growth rates in the number of foreign, private domestic and government companies, and their proportions plotted over time. Three trends are visible from Figure 3. First, the growth in the numbers of foreign firms was low, and in many cases, negative, till the late 1970s. In fact, the rates of decline from the late 1970s to the early 1980s were very substantial, for reasons that have been discussed earlier, but since then these rates have been positive. In the 1990s, these growth rates were increasing. In the post-liberalization period, the number of foreign companies operating in India has risen, on an average, by almost 8.5 per cent annually. In other words, foreign firms do seem to want to do business in India.

Second, the growth rates in the number of domestic private firms were initially negative till the early 1960s. Recollect that from the mid to late 1950s, the *commanding heights* doctrine led to the establishment of several

FIGURE 3

Growth rates in the number of different types of companies

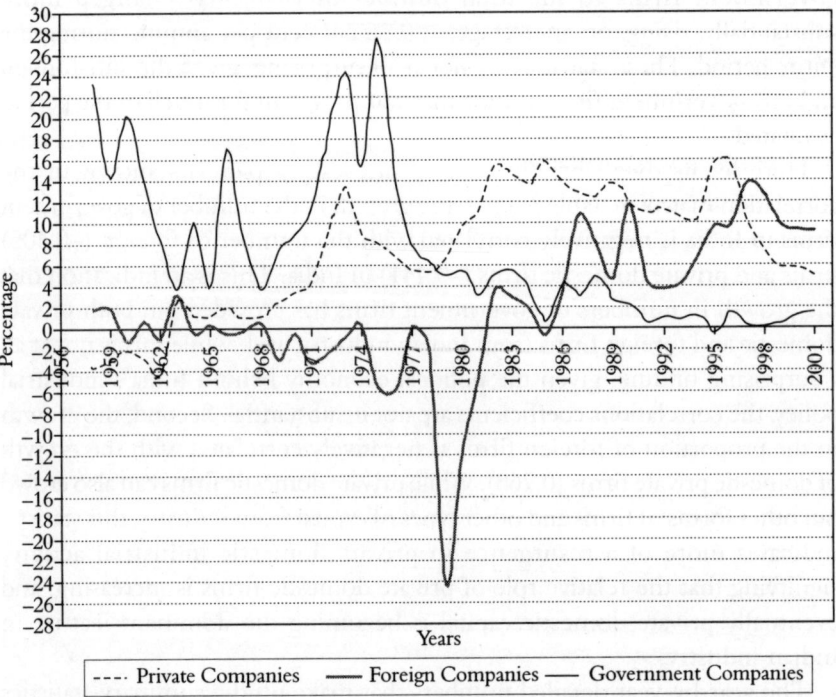

Years

---- Private Companies ——— Foreign Companies ——— Government Companies

government enterprises. This phenomenon did crowd out private enterprise, but since the 1960s, the growth rates have been positive. In fact, from the late 1970s onwards, notwithstanding the socialist economy doctrine perpetrated by the government, the growth rates have been very substantial. From 1981 till the late 1990s, the growth rates have been in the double digits and only slowed down somewhat in the twenty-first century. On the other hand, the base of firms has increased so much numerically that the annual number of new companies being established is still very substantial. In the post-liberalization period, the number of domestic companies operating in India has grown by almost 10 per cent per annum, on an average.

Third, government companies grew in number very substantially from the 1950s till the late 1970s and early 1980s. Their growth rate has substantially shrunk since then, and during the period after 1991, the number of government companies increased at an annual average rate of 0.79. The fact that this growth rate is not negative is, of course, a source of curiosity since the growth rates are expected to become negative as privatization proceeds and the number of government firms reduces. While this article

FIGURE 4

Change in the proportion of different categories of companies

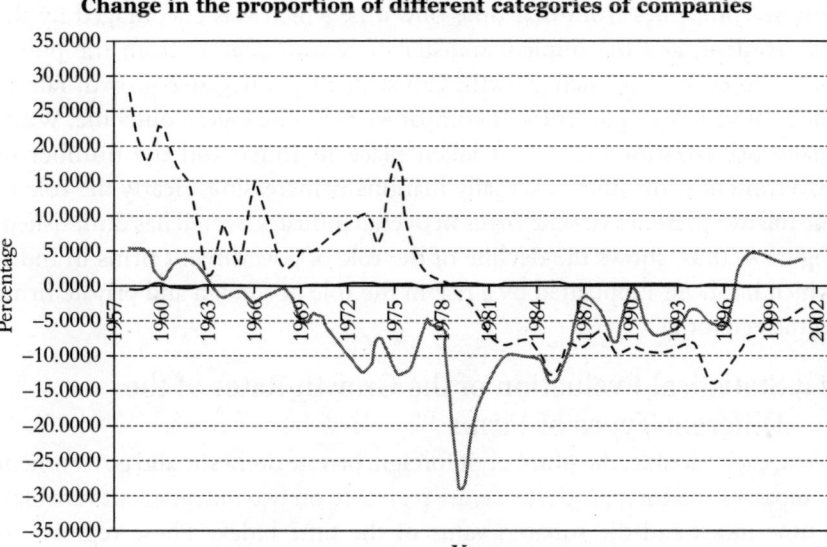

Years

| ——— Foreign Firms | ——— Domestic Firms | - - - Government Firms |

does not deal with the privatization issue as such, the finding is an indication of the lack of any success in privatization efforts in India. In fact, it is quite the opposite since the number of government companies has increased, albeit quite marginally.

Figure 4 displays the annual trends in the growth rate of the proportions that the different types or kinds of companies have to the total number of companies operating in India. Foreign companies lost their relative standing in Indian industry by the 1960s, a fact also observed by Kidron (1965), and till the mid-1990s, kept on losing it, albeit the pace of such loss was not as accelerated in the 1980s as it had been in the 1970s. It is only after the mid-1990s that their relative presence in Indian industry started increasing. Correspondingly, the change in the relative presence of domestic private firms in Indian industry has been almost negligible. The growth in the number of companies overall is mainly driven by an increase in the number of private companies, and the relative presence of the private sector has, therefore, remained constant.

On the other hand, the role of government companies in India became pronounced since the mid-1950s and this is reflected in Figure 4. The growth rates in the relative proportion of government companies to the total number of companies were positive till the late 1970s, and, since then, have turned negative. This trend is quite consistent with the growth in the number of private companies from that time onwards, which was encouraged by the government, and the implicit transfer of resources away from the public sector to encourage such growth. Consequently, a negative growth rate in the relative role of government companies is a quite logical outcome. While many privatizations have not taken place in India, and the number of government companies is actually marginally increasing, clearly the role of the relative presence of state firms in overall industry overall has diminished. Figure 4, thus, shows the decline of the role of government firms in India, which has been supplanted by a rise in the role of foreign and private firms in the economy.

2.4 Statistical Evaluation of the Growth Rates of the Different Types of Firms

Next, each variable, the number of foreign, private domestic and government companies and their proportions, are regressed on two independent variables: a time index and the squared value of the time index. These regressions permit a statistical evaluation of the significance of the growth rates of these variables. The equation is of the general form: $\Delta = \alpha + \beta t + \delta t^2 + \mu t$. The symbol Δ denotes the percentage growth rate or change for each of the six variables and t is the time index. A significantly positive value of d indicates an acceleration in the pace of change; a significantly negative value indicates deceleration.

The inclusion of time squared on the right-hand side introduces a multi-collinearity problem. This is solved by normalizing time in mean deviation form, that is, it is set to zero on the mid-point of the time series. This normalization makes time and its square orthogonal. The normalization of time only affects β. The estimate of δ and its standard error are invariant with respect to the normalization. In the log-quadratic estimation, the value of β is the same as in the log-linear model. The standard error of β is the measure of instability of the growth rate of efficiency. If it is assumed that the log-quadratic form is a better estimator of the true trends in the growth rate of efficiency, and the instability measure of β is also improved, since systematic specification errors are cleansed from the data. The results are given in Table 4.

Table 4 shows that all the variables are statistically significant at the usual levels. There has been a significant acceleration in the growth in numbers of foreign and private domestic companies in India, and a significant deceleration in the growth in the number of government companies. Similarly, there has been a significant acceleration in growth in the

TABLE 4

Analysis of growth in the numbers and proportions of various types of firms

	Coefficient estimates (standard errors in parentheses)	Coefficient estimates (standard errors in parentheses)	Coefficient estimates (standard errors in parentheses)
Panel A	Numbers of foreign companies	Numbers of government companies	Numbers of private companies
Intercept	297.932*** (38.332)	0.522*** (30.364)	−1926.360*** (8756.363)
Growth	4.104*** (1.300)	33.309*** (1.029)	109.709*** (296.975)
Acceleration	0.959*** (0.114)	−0.237** (0.090)	5.577*** (26.67)
R^2	0.661	0.962	0.977
Panel B	Proportion of foreign companies	Proportion of government companies	Proportion of private companies
Intercept	2.152*** (0.094)	1.289*** (0.063)	91.520*** (0.185)
Growth	−0.058*** (0.003)	−0.007*** (0.002)	0.172*** (0.006)
Acceleration	0.001** (0.000)	−0.002*** (0.000)	0.002*** (0.000)
R^2	0.889	0.805	0.949

Source: Author's computations.
Notes: *** $p < 0.01$; ** $p < 0.05$; * $p < 0.10$.

proportions of foreign and private domestic companies within Indian industry, and a significant deceleration in the proportion of government companies. These results provide statistical support for all the other trends that have been described and discussed so far.

3. Assessment of Economic Performance

The evidence reveals a fairly complex pattern of foreign firm dynamics. Foreign firms, which were once prominent in India before Independence, became an extremely limited part of India's economy but since 1991, they have been entering India in large numbers. What does this signify? What has been the impact of their presence on India's industrial performance over the entire time period being studied? These are important questions lying at the very heart of the issues as to how India's industrial structure has evolved so far, and will evolve in the future. In a sense, the *raison d'etre* of this article is to evaluate the long-run relationships between the presence, be it increasing or decreasing, of foreign firms in the Indian economy and the productivity of its industrial sector; this section describes the analysis carried out in this respect.

Data from the DCA on the growth of the corporate sector are next matched with the ASI data to evaluate these questions. For the period 1957–58 to 2001–02, the data generated by the ASI in India are used to calculate a measure of industrial performance and competitiveness, which is expressed as relative productive efficiency. Variations in the measure of productive efficiency are then explained by using the growth in the numbers and proportions of the various types of companies as independent variables within the framework of time series regressions. The ASI data relate to the organized sector of the manufacturing industry and have seen prior use (Majumdar 1996). See the Appendix at the end of the article for more details.

The ASI data relate to the organized sector of the manufacturing industry and have seen prior use. The factory sector summary is used as the data source for this study. From the data set, labour and capital inputs as well as output measures can be identified. The advantage of using this data is that information for the entire Indian industry is available. The characteristic of this particular database is that, the data are aggregate because of the reporting policies of the Department of Statistics of the Government of India. However, the aggregation issue is unavoidable since information on a key variable, on firm level employment, is not available for private sector firms from any source whatsoever, particularly for over a long time series. In fact, the availability of employment data is one of the unique strengths of the ASI system. Hence, any comparative study of efficiency and performance has to use a database such as this. Aggregate data also helps prevent any biases in the sample selection since data pertaining to the entire industrial population is considered for comparative efficiency assessment purposes.

The ASI coverage and the almost five decades of time series data yield rich information on the entire population of enterprises that make up the organized industrial sector of India, and the data generated by the ASI constitute the most crucial component of industrial statistics in India. According to the Department of Statistics, the industrial sector is broadly classified into the organized and unorganized sectors. These institutional categories are found in all the three major groups of industries, namely, mining and quarrying, manufacturing, and electricity generation, transmission and distribution. The ASI covers organized segments of the last two groups, and excludes mining and quarrying from its purview. Services and activities such as cold storage, water supply, and the repair of motor vehicles and of other durable goods, are also covered under the survey, as they are incidental to the manufacturing process.

The ASI does not cover the unorganized or unregistered manufacturing sector of Indian industry. The ASI, however, covers all factories registered under Sections 2 m (i) and 2 m (ii) of the Factories Act, 1948, which are factories employing 10 or more workers with the aid of power and those employing 20 or more workers without the aid of power, respectively, on any day of the preceding 12 months. The ASI frame of reference is based on the list of registered factories maintained by the Chief Inspector of Factories (CIF) in each state, and those maintained by licensing authorities for indigenous tobacco and cigar establishments, and electricity undertakings. The ASI frame gets revised from time to time by the deletion of de-registered factories and the inclusion of newly registered ones. Initially, the ASI was being revised once every two years until 1981–82. Between 1982–83 and 1988–89, the frame was revised once in four years. From 1989-90 onwards, the frame is being revised once in three years. But new registrations are added in the existing frame every year, and the regional offices of the Field Operations Directorate (FOD) of the CSO, which maintain a close liaison with the offices of CIF in the states, update the frame every year.

3.1 Variables for Calculating Efficiency

In the calculation of the relative productive efficiency parameters, four inputs and one output are used in the computation of a productive efficiency index for each observation. The inputs are: deflated rupee values of fixed capital, deflated working capital, actual number of workers employed, and the actual number of managerial staff employed. The double deflation method for indexing is not used, as it is extremely controversial. The creation of value necessitates the acquisition and configuration of capabilities, which are encapsulated in physical, liquid and human capital. Capital inputs, both physical and working capital, are expressed in terms of crores of rupees. Human capital inputs are expressed in terms of thousands of employees. Fixed capital, measured as gross capital, apart from plant and machinery, covers all other types of assets deployed for production, transportation, living or recreational facilities, and hospitals and schools for factory personnel. It includes assets of the owning enterprise's head office allocable to the factory and also the full value of the assets taken on a hire-purchase basis, excluding the interest element; it excludes intangible assets solely used for post-manufacturing activities such as sale, storage, and distribution.

The output variable used is net value added, also expressed in terms of crores of rupees, which is a standard measure of the firm level output. In the literature on efficiency measurement, both value added and gross output are used to measure output. However, Griliches and Ringstad (1971) advance arguments in favour of using value added because it facilitates a comparison of results for firms which may be heterogeneous in material consumption. Second, the inclusion of material as an input may lead to the problem that all variation in efficiency may be captured by materials consumption, thus obscuring the role of physical and human capital utilization.

A further choice arises between the uses of either gross or net value added as the output measure. Denison (1974) makes a case for the use of net value added on theoretical grounds by arguing that, since gross value added includes a measure of capital consumption, there is no rationale as to why capital consumption ought to be maximized rather than minimized. Nevertheless, value added captures the hybrid aspects of firms' activities. First, it captures a production relationship between primary factors and output. This relationship is based on the capabilities of managements. Second, it also captures a profit-generating relationship between firm-specific capital and the output of firms, which, while also being dependent on endogenous management capabilities, is highly dependent on exogenous demand and supply conditions.

The performance measure described below is a measure of resource utilization and not period-to-period changes in resource consumption that would be generated by fitting a production function. Fitting a production function requires that all inputs be included; otherwise the production function is under-specified. It has not been possible to acquire data for the time period concerned for raw material and energy inputs so as to estimate a fully specified cost or production function. The time series data are just not available. The use of the efficiency estimation method adopted enables relative efficiency measures to be calculated since a cost or production function, relying on a particular statistical form, is not estimated. The resulting efficiency scores provide a measure of relative performance in the utilization of these inputs. Since these two inputs are the most critical within the manufacturing industry, the efficiency estimate captures the principal components of performance of the manufacturing industry.

3.2 Estimation of Efficiency

The Data Envelopment Analysis (DEA) has been used for estimation purposes. An extensive literature has evolved on the topic of DEA (see Charnes et al. 1994). This article does not go into much detail other than to state that the algorithm used for analysis in Majumdar (1996) is also used in this evaluation. Using observed output and input data, and without making any assumptions as to the nature of the underlying technology or functional form, the DEA algorithm calculates an ex-post measure of the comparative efficiency of each observation. This is accomplished by constructing an empirically-based frontier, and by evaluating each observation against all others in the data set.

The DEA performs optimization for each individual observation, in place of the overall aggregation and single optimization performed in statistical regressions. Instead of trying to fit a regression plane through the centre of the data, the DEA floats a piece-wise linear surface to rest on top of the observations. This is empirically-driven by data, rather than by assumptions as to functional forms. The only assumption made is that the piece-wise linear envelopment surface is convex. Next, the efficiency score is a bounded efficiency measure, and any observation with a score of less than 1 has a measurable potential for improvement. This is an important quality, as the relative performance differences between observations can be easily understood.

3.3 Analysis of the Efficiency Patterns

The annual efficiency parameters calculated are displayed in Figure 5. The descriptive statistics for the efficiency parameters that have been calculated are given in Table 5. Let us first discuss the pattern of the annual efficiency scores and then the statistics. A reiteration of what the efficiency scores mean is in order. These are comparative efficiency scores evaluating the relative productive efficiency of each observation against all other observations. The efficiency for each year is evaluated against all other years, and the results display the comparative efficiency position.

Figure 5 shows that the efficiency scores for the first part of the overall period were at 1; in other words, these years were the frontier definers. The scores of 1 are observed for the years 1957–58 to 1961–62. After that period, efficiency in the Indian industry plummeted. There are two possible explanations for this. One is the impact of the commanding heights policy regime, put into place in the mid to late 1950s, which was having a lagged impact on performance. The second is that this period was the aftermath of the Indo-China War of 1962, when a very difficult foreign exchange situation arose and a deteriorating situation in the agricultural sector led to a decline in effective demand since the rural sector wages and incomes, which were quite important then, dropped sharply.

Productive efficiency continued to plummet till the early 1970s. By that time, the efficiency of Indian industry was just three-fourths of what it had

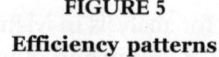

FIGURE 5
Efficiency patterns

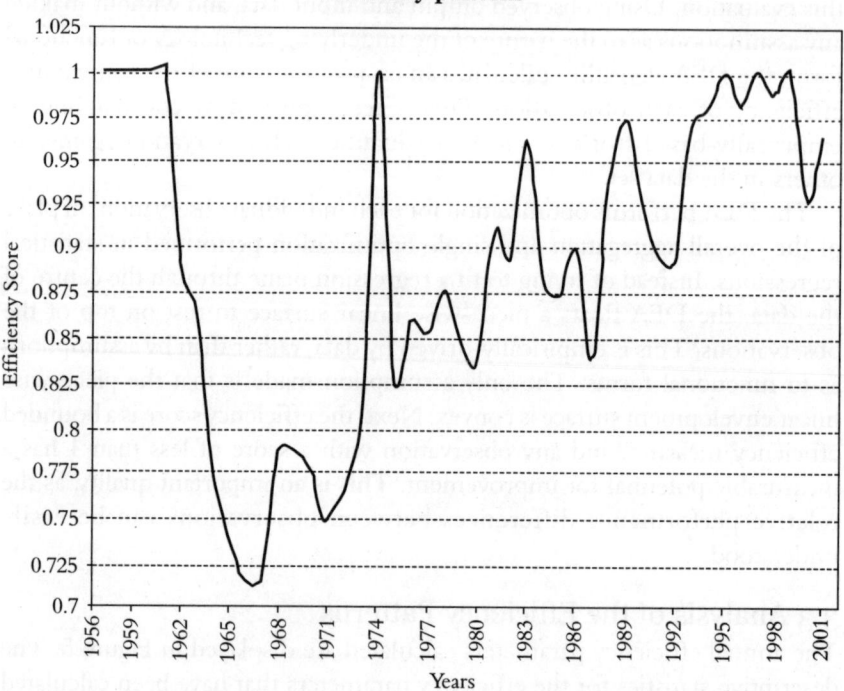

been less than a decade ago. There was a rising efficiency trend thereafter, but even by the early 1980s, productive efficiency was just 85 per cent of what it had been in the late 1950s. A major catch-up with the past commenced in the early 1980s, and was achieved in the 1990s. This trend has also been noted elsewhere (Ahluwalia 1985; Majumdar 1996). Thus, the productive efficiency picture for India over five decades is almost U-shaped, in its simplest representation, and the temporal pattern is stationary. The statistics given in Table 5 are discussed below.

The overall average efficiency score for the entire period, 1957–58 to 2001–02, is 0.896. This period is divided into four phases or sub-periods, reflecting the mindsets and attitudes that prevailed during each of those periods, and the efficiency scores relevant for that period are discussed. The first phase ranges from 1957–58 to 1971–72. This is the period between the commencement of the commanding heights economy and before the commencement of the FERA period in 1973. During this period, the average efficiency score was 0.854. The variations in efficiency were also the largest during this period. During the next period, ranging from 1973–74 to 1979–80,

TABLE 5

Descriptive statistics of efficiency patterns

Years	Average	Standard deviation	Coefficient of variation
1957–58 to 2001–02			
The period as a whole	0.896	0.088	0.098
Phase 1—1957–58 to 1971–72			
From commanding heights to FERA	0.854	0.116	0.137
Phase 2—1973–74 to 1979–80			
From FERA to the end of confusion	0.867	0.063	0.072
Phase 3—1980–81 to 1990–91			
From enlightenment to sudden crisis	0.904	0.045	0.050
Phase 4—1991–92 to 2001–02			
From liberalization till today	0.964	0.039	0.041

Source: Author's computations.
Notes: *** $p < 0.01$; ** $p < 0.05$; * $p < 0.10$.

the average efficiency score was 0.867. This is the period after the commencement of FERA in 1973 and before the commencement of any sort of reforms. During the mid to late 1970s, there was also a period when civil liberties were put on hold and the party that had ruled from Independence lost its power. The average scores for both these periods are much less than the average score for the overall period.

The early 1980s signify the period when the withdrawal of some of the more draconian and egregious policies commenced, with the government desiring to promote private enterprise in a substantial way. There are two sub-periods. One of these is from 1980–81 to 1990–91. This is a phase when enlightenment dawned till the foreign exchange crisis of 1991 brought about a complete change in mindsets. During this particular period, the government of Mrs Indira Gandhi attempted to introduce reforms by stealth while the successor government of Rajiv Gandhi attempted reforms with reluctance (Bhagwati 1993). The average efficiency score during this period is 0.904, reflecting productive efficiency growth and a catch-up with the past. The final period commences from 1991–92, after the initiation of reforms, till 2001–02. The average efficiency score for this sub-period is 0.964, reflecting a considerable growth in productive efficiency in Indian industry after the commencement of the reforms. In addition, the variations in efficiency during this period are the least of any of the four sub-periods.

3.4 Time Series Regression Analysis of the Data

In order to evaluate the long-run relationship between the presence of foreign firms in India and the productive efficiency of Indian industry, while controlling for the presence of private domestic firms as well as government firms, a series of time series regressions are estimated in which the dependent variable is the annual productive efficiency score and the explanatory variables are the changes in the numbers and proportions of the different types of companies. This approach is predicated by the estimates of an auto-regressive integrated moving average (ARIMA) model, which suggests non-stationarity in the explanatory variables.

Initially, ordinary least squares (OLS) regressions for the model are estimated wherein the explanatory variables represent the changes in the numbers of the various types of companies, including foreign, private domestic and government. The dependent variable is that of productive efficiency over time. An OLS model also includes the past value of performance to control for endogeneity, and these results are similar to the model excluding the past values of performance. The auto-regressive conditional heteroscedasticity (ARCH) tests (Engle 1982) reject the null hypothesis of homoscedasticity. Thereafter, the generalized auto-regressive conditional heteroscedasticity (GARCH) models (Bollerlsev 1986) are estimated to evaluate the long-run relationship between productive efficiency and changes in the presence of foreign firms in India. The results of these estimations are provided in Table 6.

The first column shows that the growth in the number of foreign firms operating in India is significantly ($p < 0.001$) and positively associated with the productive efficiency in the long run. When the growth in the number of government companies is introduced as a control, the results stay robust. The growth in the number of government companies is, however, negatively and significantly associated with the long-run productive efficiency of Indian industry. This is not an unexpected result, given the widespread view that, in general, government firms are less superior in performance to private firms, irrespective of whether these private firms are of domestic or foreign origin.

Columns (4) and (5) of Table 6 now include three important control variables that can have an effect on long-run productivity. Using time series data put together from various sources, such as the Reserve Bank of India (RBI) and the Government of India, the control variables calculated are: the level of foreign exchange reserves, growth in GNP at factor cost, and the level of net invisibles in the Indian economy. These factors control for key aspects of the macroeconomic environment that can affect manufacturing performance (Joshi and Little 1994). Also, variations in these variables will reflect the significant policy changes that have taken place over the period studied.

TABLE 6

GARCH estimates of relationships between the growth in numbers of various types of firms and performance measured as productive efficiency

	Coefficient estimate (standard error)	Coefficient estimate (standard error)	Coefficient estimate (standard error)	Coefficient estimate (standard error)
Mean Equation				
Intercept	91.271***	92.946***	51.911***	84.510***
	(0.749)	(1.046)	(5.258)	(1.770)
Growth in number of foreign firms	0.437***	0.388***	0.238***	0.155*
	(0.092)	(0.092)	(0.078)	(0.091)
Growth in number of private firms			0.560***	0.607***
			(0.124)	(0.137)
Growth in number of government firms		−0.338**	0.070	−0.143
		(0.164)	(0.144)	(0.160)
Foreign exchange reserves			3.669***	
			(0.585)	
Growth in GNP at factor cost			−0.044	0.183
			(0.180)	(0.205)
Net invisibles				0.001***
				(0.000)
Variance Equation				
Alpha	12.134	3.040	6.494*	4.516
	(9.132)	(3.489)	(3.515)	(3.597)
Alpha	0.667*	0.483*	0.816**	0.722**
	(0.343)	(0.289)	(0.341)	(0.311)
Phi	0.094	0.434*	0.047	0.163
	(0.282)	(0.229)	(0.112)	(0.150)
Delta	8.269	18.777	26.169	24.428
	(8.253)	(16.300)	(19.55)	(18.52)
Log likelihood	−141.33	−140.180	−131.92	−134.60

Source: Author's computations.
Notes: *** $p < 0.01$; ** $p < 0.05$; * $p < 0.10$.

In Column (4) of Table 6, the level of foreign exchange reserves and growth in GNP at factor cost are introduced as controls. The growth in the number of private domestic firms is also introduced as a control variable. The results stay robust. The variable for the private firms is also positive and significant, implying that there is a dynamic productivity effect of the growth of domestic entrepreneurship in India. In Column (5) of the Table 6, the growth in GNP at factor cost and the level of net invisibles, along with the growth in the number of domestic private firms, are introduced as control variables. The results stay robust.

4. Assessment and Implications

The results show that a strong long-run relationship exists between the growing presence of foreign firms in India and the productive efficiency of Indian industry as a whole. Therefore, the notion that foreign firms' capabilities can spill over to other sectors of industry does find support in the overall data. Hence, the primary conclusion is that past efforts to limit the presence of foreign firms in India were short-sighted, to say the least. Even more short-sighted was the encouragement of the growth of government firms within Indian industry. Their growing presence, because of a crowding out effect, has had a deleterious effect as revealed by the long-run negative relationship between the growth of government firms and the productive efficiency for Indian industry as a whole. While privatization is a favoured solution to deal with government firms in India, it has hardly taken place. One option is to let the government firms eventually wither away with time. Nevertheless, a detailed statement of what needs to be done with the public sector is outside the scope of this article.

There cannot, thus, be any doubt that encouraging the growth of foreign firms in India, via the encouragement of foreign direct investment (FDI), is a critical policy contingency that needs to be implemented. Foreign firms, relative to private domestic firms, and most certainly, relative to government firms, have a significant positive impact on India's industrial performance. Yet, even though the presence of foreign firms and foreign direct investment is growing in India, the relative proportion of foreign firms to the total number of firms is very small. Table 7 lists the number of foreign firms, the proportion of foreign firms to the total number of firms, the growth rates in the number of firms, and the growth rates in the proportion of foreign firms to the total for the period after 1991. These are some of the basic data that have already been analysed.

First, the number of foreign firms in India increased very substantially in the decade or so for which the data are presented in Table 7. The proportion for foreign firms to the total number of firms, however, dropped. This is, no doubt, because of the extraordinary unleashing of domestic private entrepreneurial activity in India, as a consequence of which the number of private firms being established is increasing at a substantial rate as all the evidence indicates. Thus, the number of private domestic firms tends to overwhelm the number of foreign firms. Nevertheless, since the analysis shows the superior technological and other capabilities hypothesis associated with foreign firms to be valid, there are further substantial latent productivity gains to be made by Indian industry if the number of foreign firms operating in India does increase.

TABLE 7

Growth rates in the post-liberalization period of the numbers and proportions of foreign firms operating in India

Year	Number of foreign firms operating in India	Percentage of foreign firms to the total number of firms in India	Growth in the number of foreign firms in India	Growth in the proportion of foreign firms in India
1991–92	489	0.215 per cent	4.26 per cent	–6.02 per cent
1992–93	507	0.200 per cent	3.68 per cent	–6.96 per cent
1993–94	529	0.189 per cent	4.33 per cent	–5.57 per cent
1994–95	565	0.183 per cent	6.80 per cent	–3.19 per cent
1995–96	619	0.174 per cent	9.55 per cent	–5.12 per cent
1996–97	679	0.165 per cent	9.69 per cent	–5.19 per cent
1997–98	772	0.170 per cent	13.69 per cent	3.19 per cent
1998–99	871	0.178 per cent	12.82 per cent	5.03 per cent
1999–00	956	0.185 per cent	9.75 per cent	3.87 per cent
2000–01	1,045	0.191 per cent	9.30 per cent	3.18 per cent
2001–02	1,141	0.199 per cent	9.18 per cent	4.07 per cent

Source: Author's computations based on DCA data as included in column (1).

On this score, Table 7 shows that the growth in the number of foreign firms in India has been substantial during the post-1991 period. In fact, the growth in numbers averages 8.5 per cent for the period, ranging from 1991–92 to 2001–02, but the growth since 1995–96 has been at over 10 per cent per year. Even the proportion of foreign firms to the total number of firms, which dropped from 1991–92 to 1996–97, shows a positive growth during the period from 1997–98 onwards. Some of this decline was due to the resurgence of private domestic entrepreneurial activity in India. Yet, the positive growth in the proportions seen after the mid-1990s portends an interest in India by the suppliers of foreign capital. Thus, foreign firms are becoming an increasing presence in the Indian economy.

4.1 The Importance of Property Rights
What is therefore right and what is still not right? The ambiguity and ambivalence that India has displayed towards foreign investment, especially from the early 1970s onwards, has been replaced by a change of spirit. Or has it? The first important property rights policy change was the automatic approval for foreign firms to hold 51 per cent ownership. Hitherto, foreign firms could hold up to 40 per cent shares and the permission to hold 51 per cent was given, quite grudgingly, in a few cases. Earlier work (Chhibber and Majumdar 1999) had highlighted that only when foreign firms have 51 per cent ownership, do Indian companies display superior profitability. This is explained by the notion that superior performance is a function of the superior capabilities that foreign firms possess, and which they will be loath

to transfer to India unless they hold majority ownership in Indian companies. Thus, the automatic availability of property rights has been a major change that affects the incentives of foreign firms to set up operations in India.

The second change related to property rights has been the extension of automatic approvals for having ownership stakes of up to 74 per cent in all but a few sectors such as media and telecommunications. This took place in 1997. As a consequence, in 1997–98, the number of foreign firms operating in India grew by over 13 per cent, and it was also during this year that a positive growth in the proportion of foreign firms to the total number of firms was noted. Thus, basic property rights changes have had significant effects in terms of providing incentives for foreign firms to operate in India. Yet, policy pronouncements have to be consistent so that encouragement for entry is material.

4.2 Loss of Nerve and Policy Inconsistency

A policy paradox, which has had unfortunate consequences, has also been perpetrated. The various policy measures on liberalization have been influenced by Indian entrepreneurs. For a long time, during the period of the closed economy, they had virtual monopolies under the licensing system. Previously, the government had taken a decision on the entry of foreign firms into India and the maximum shareholding they could hold. Such discretion was taken away by allowing automatic entry, yet simultaneously the Indian government managed to give the veto rights to the Indian private sector on certain aspects of the entry of foreign firms into India by promulgating Press Note 18 in late 1998.

At the time of the Note, a coalition government had taken power. One of its constituent planks was that of *Swadeshi,* an expression evoking the existence of purely domestic industry. A crisis of confidence among Indian entrepreneurs could have arisen since a large body of firms had gotten used to operating within a closed system with no competition. As a result, there were pressures to have this note promulgated. This seems surprising, given that private domestic firms were being established in large numbers after 1991. Conversely, the pro-protection lobby, called the Bombay Group (Das 2002), could have had its ideas implemented by appealing to the *Swadeshi* lobby, which would then have organized the issue of Press Note 18. Nevertheless, this note signalled significant inconsistencies on the part of the government which simultaneously sought to encourage foreign investment and then control its disposition.

According to Press Note 18, if foreign investors planning entry had a previous joint venture, technology transfer or trade mark agreement in the same or a related field in India, they could not use the automatic route for a new joint venture or technology transfer agreement and would have to apply specifically for new investment in another enterprise. Thus further *de novo* enterprises could be established but additional collaborations could not be entered into with other partners. Second, the foreign investor would have to justify to the Foreign Investment Promotion Board how the new proposal would not jeopardize the interests of the existing joint venture or technology partner.

The psychological implications of this pronouncement are quite profound. A signal clearly sent is that the Indian partners were lacking in confidence and wanted to retain control rights, using the government as a proxy to decide how foreign firms could conduct their business strategies in India. The note also caused concern among foreign investors, since it put substantial power in the hands of Indian private sector industrialists, who already had relationships with foreign companies, in that they could effectively prevent foreign investors coming into India even if their own joint venture were not doing well. It is difficult to speculate on the precise numbers of foreign companies scared off by this note, but given that India's annual FDI levels have been comparatively low, in financial terms, the number could be quite large. The note was repealed in early 2005, showing a recovery of nerve on the part of the government. Nevertheless, the impact of the note is likely to have been of some consequence. Subsequent analysis and research can evaluate the impact of this press note on retarding FDI into India between 1999 and 2005.

5. Conclusion

This article evaluates whether the changing presence of foreign firms in the corporate sector has had an impact on the long-run economic performance of India's industry. For this purpose, the patterns of corporate demography in India from the 1950s to the 2000s have been traced, using a data set put together from the Department of Company Affairs (DCA) of the Government of India that covers the numbers of the various types of companies making up India's corporate sector. For measuring performance, the productive efficiency indices for the entire Indian industry have been calculated by using a database put together by the Central Statistical Organization as the Annual Survey of Industries (ASI). The DCA and ASI data cover the period from 1957–58 to 2001–02, and permit an economy-wide analysis for a period of five decades.

There are three important findings. The results show a strong relationship between the growing presence of foreign firms in India and the productive efficiency of Indian industry. They also indicate that the notion that foreign firms' capabilities can spill over to other sectors of industry finds support. Past efforts to limit the presence of foreign firms in India were short-sighted, and even more short-sighted was the support given towards encouraging the growth of government firms in India. Their growing presence was associated with a strong long-run negative relationship with productive efficiency for Indian industry as a whole.

During the period following the commencement of reforms in 1991, the number of foreign firms in India has increased very substantially. This growth in numbers averages 8.5 per cent for the period from 1991–92 to 2001–02, and since 1995–96, it has been at over 10 per cent per year. While the proportion for foreign firms to the total number of firms dropped, no doubt because of the unleashing of domestic private entrepreneurial activity in India, this statistic shows a positive growth during the period from 1997–98 onwards. This positive growth in the proportions after the mid-1990s portends a significant interest in India shown by the suppliers of foreign capital. Thus, foreign firms are interested in increasing their presence in the Indian economy, with positive performance consequences expected from such increased participation.

So far, basic property rights changes have had significant effects on providing incentives for foreign firms to operate in India and the automatic availability of such rights has been a major factor affecting the motivation of foreign firms to operate in India. Yet, policy pronouncements have not been consistent. The Indian government also gave veto rights to the Indian private sector on certain aspects of foreign firm entry into India by promulgating Press Note 18 in late 1998. It is difficult to speculate on the precise number of foreign companies that were scared off by this note. Although the note was repealed in early 2005, yet other roadblocks remain. Future research is necessary to evaluate the impact that Press Note 18 might have had on retarding the growth in the number of foreign firms in India, and thereby, its long-run industrial performance.

Appendix: Details of the Annual Survey of Industries Data

The history of industrial statistics in India unfolds as follows. Although the first Factories Act was enacted in India in 1881 and revised in 1891, 1911, 1922 and 1934, the importance of collecting comprehensive industrial statistics was not realized until 1942. The Industrial Statistics Act, 1942 was passed in that year and it empowered the Government of India to collect various industrial statistics from establishments registered under the then Indian Factories Act, 1934. The Directorate of Industrial Statistics was set up in 1945 to coordinate and supervise the collection of statistics through industrial census operations and to compile and publish their results. An annual census of 29 industry groups of these 63 groups was conducted from 1946 to 1956 under the provisions of the Industrial Statistics Act of 1942 and the Census of Manufacturing Industries (CMI) Rules of 1945 framed thereunder.

On the basis of the recommendations of the National Income Committee, a Sample Survey of Manufacturing Industries (SSMI) was started in 1950 covering all the 63 industry groups on a sample basis. Subsequent to the passing of the Collection of Statistics Act, 1953, which replaced the Industrial Statistics Act of 1942 in 1956, the CMI continued on a voluntary basis for the years 1957 and 1958. The SSMI also continued up to 1958. All the reports from the manufacturing census from 1946 to 1958 were published. Although the CMI covered factories employing 20 or more workers by using power in any manufacturing process, there has been year-to-year variation in the geographical area covered and the response rate. The CMI published information on capital (fixed capital, working capital and depreciation), employment (workers and persons other than workers), man-hours, payment to each category of employees along with the value of benefits and privileges, inputs (fuels, materials and total), the value of output of products and by-products, and net value added.

Although the Collection of Statistics Act of 1953 came into force on November 10, 1956, the Collection of Statistics (Central) Rules framed under the same Act came to be notified in January 1960, providing for a comprehensive Annual Survey of Industries (ASI) in India from 1959 onwards. Thus, the ASI replaced both the CMI and SSMI from that year onwards. Since 1959, the survey is being conducted annually under the statutory provisions of the 1953 Act and 1959 Rules, except in Jammu and Kashmir, where it is conducted under the state Collection of Statistics Act 1961 and the rules framed thereunder in 1964. The ASI extends to the entire country except the states of Arunachal Pradesh, Mizoram, Sikkim and the Union Territory of Lakshadweep.

Sumit K. Majumdar, School of Management, University of Texas at Dallas, Richardson, TX 75083. Email: majumdar@utdallas.edu

References

Ahluwalia, I.J. 1985. *Industrial Growth in India: Stagnation Since the Mid-Sixties*. Delhi: Oxford University Press.

Athreye, S. and S. Kapur. 2001. 'Private Foreign Investment in India: Pain or Panacea?', *World Economy*, 24(3): 399–424.

Bagchi, A.K. 1972. *Private Investment in India, 1900 to 1939*. Cambridge: Cambridge University Press.

Balasubramanyam, V. N., M. Salisu and D. Sapsford. 1996. 'Foreign Direct Investment and Growth in EP and IS Countries', *Economic Journal*, 106(434): 96–105.

Bhagwati, J.N. 1993. *India in Transition: Freeing the Economy*. Oxford: Oxford University Press.

Blomstrom M. and A. Kokko. 1998. 'Multinational Corporations and Spillovers', *Journal of Economic Surveys*, 12(3): 247–77.

Bollerslev, T. 1986. 'Generalized Auto-regressive Conditional Heteroscedasticity', *Journal of Econometrics*, 31(3): 307–27.

Buckley, P.J. and M. Casson. 1976. *The Future of the Multinational Enterprise*. London: Macmillan.

Carroll, G.R. and M.T. Hannan. 2000. *The Demography of Corporations and Industries*. NJ: Princeton University Press.

Caves, R.E. 1996. *Multinational Enterprise and Economic Analysis*. Cambridge: Cambridge University Press, Second edition.

Charnes, A., W.W. Cooper, A. Lewin and L. Seiford. 1994. *Data Envelopment Analysis: Theory, Methodology and Applications*. Boston: Kluwer.

Chhibber, P.K. and S.K. Majumdar. 1999. 'Foreign Ownership and Profitability: Property Rights, Control and the Performance of Firms in Indian Industry', *Journal of Law and Economics*, 52(1): 209–38.

Das, G. 2002. *India Unbound*. New York: Profile Books.

de la Torre, J. 1974. 'Foreign Investment and Export Dependence', *Economic Development and Cultural Change*, 23(1): 133–50.

de Soto, H. 2000. *The Mystery of Capital*. New York: Basic Books.

Denison, E.F. 1974. *Accounting for United States Economic Growth, 1929 to 1969*. Washington, DC: The Brookings Institution.

Dunning, J. 1993. *Multinational Enterprises and the Global Economy*. Don Mills, Ont.: Addison-Wesley.

Engle, R.F. 1982. 'Auto-regressive Conditional Heteroscedasticity with Estimates of the Variance of UK Inflation', *Econometrica*, 50(5): 987–1008.

Feinberg, S. and S.K. Majumdar. 2001. 'Technology Spillovers from Foreign Direct Investment in the Indian Pharmaceutical Industry', *Journal of International Business Studies*, 32(3): 421–37.

Gorg, H. and E. Strobl. 2001. 'Multinational Corporations and Productivity Spillovers: A Meta-Analysis', *Economic Journal*, 111(475): 723–39.

Government of India. 1985. *Seventh Five Year Plan*. New Delhi.

Griliches, Z. and V. Ringstad. 1971. *Economies of Scale and the Form of the Production Function*. Amsterdam: North-Holland.

Helleiner, G.K. 1988. 'Introduction', in G.K. Helleiner (ed.), *Trade Policy, Industrialisation and Development*. Oxford: Clarendon Press.

Helpman, E. 1984. 'A Simple Theory of International Trade with Multinational Corporations', *Journal of Political Economy*, 92(3): 451–71.

Hymer, S. 1976. *The International Operations of National Firms: A Study of Direct Foreign Investment*. Cambridge: The MIT Press.

Jalan, B. 1991. *India's Economic Crisis: The Way Ahead*. New Delhi: Oxford University Press.

Joshi, V. and I.M.D. Little. 1994. *India: Macroeconomics and Political Economy, 1964–1991*. Oxford: Oxford University Press.

Kidron, M. 1965. *Foreign Investments in India*. Oxford: Oxford University Press.

Majumdar, S.K. 1996. 'Government Policies and Industrial Performance: An Institutional Analysis of the Indian Experience', *Journal of Institutional and Theoretical Economics*, 152(2): 380–411.
——.1998. 'Assessing Comparative Efficiency of the State-owned, Mixed, and Private Sectors in Indian Industry', *Public Choice*, 96(1–2): 1–24.